Rags to Riches

by
Tom Leding

TLM Publishing
Tulsa, Oklahoma

Unless otherwise indicated, all Scripture quotations are taken from the *King James Version of the Bible* (KJV). Other quotations are from *The Living Bible Paraphrased* (TLB), (Wheaton, Ill: Tyndale House Publishers, 1971); *The Amplified Bible* (Amp), (Grand Rapids: Zondervan Publishing House, 1965); *The New English Bible* (NEB), (London, England: Oxford University Press, Cambridge University Press, 1961); *The New International Version* (NIV), (Grand Rapids: Zondervan Publishing House, 1973, 1978, 1984); *New American Standard Bible* (NAS), (La Habra, CA: The Lockman Foundation, 1960-1977).

Rags to Riches
ISBN 0-9639956-4-2
Copyright © 1996 by
Tom Leding
TLM Publishing
4412 S. Harvard
Tulsa, OK 74135

Contents

Dedication

This work is dedicated in love to my son Ron Leding.

Jesus said in John 8:31,32:

Then said Jesus to those Jews which believed on him, If ye continue in my word, then are ye my disciples indeed; and ye shall know the truth, and the truth shall make you free.

It is my belief that anyone who reads the verses in this book and believes in the truth of the Word of God will be healed and will prosper.

Introduction:
What Is Prosperity?

The original "rags to riches" story of the universe is the story of mankind. The race of Adam was a poverty-stricken family line wearing "filthy rags" of righteousness (Isa. 64:6), poor in spirit, and lean of soul. Then came the wealthy God-Man Jesus, who brought His brothers and sisters an inheritance of eternal riches.

There is much discussion these days as to whether or not Jesus redeemed us from poverty when He atoned for our sins, with two main views of poverty and prosperity:

1. There are those who believe they are being humbled by being poor. Others believe that somehow God gets glory by their lack. The end result in both cases is to remain in physical poverty in a kind of reverse pride: proud of being so humble.

However, His Word tells us what gives God glory, and it is not lack. In Romans 4:20, talking about Abraham, Paul wrote: **He staggered not at the promise of God through unbelief; but was strong in faith, giving *glory* to God.** If we want to give glory to God, we must *be strong in faith* through believing God's promises.

5

2. On the other hand, there are those whose minds are permeated with the thinking of the world systems. This kind of thinking makes natural wealth a god in itself.

In recent years, much right teaching on faith for finances, health, and material gain has become permeated with worldly attitudes toward riches and possessions. Faith is judged in many circles by whether or not a person has possessions. At the opposite extreme from those who "glory" in poverty, these Christians measure spirituality *by* possessions.

This is the same kind of spiritual pride and attitude toward riches the Pharisees had in Jesus' day. There came a time, within a generation after His death and resurrection, when all of their material possessions that supposedly proved how "spiritual" they were, and how much God approved of them, were totally destroyed.

The right perspective is a balance between those two attitudes. God's provision of prosperity involves a two-fold understanding: 1) making Jesus Lord of *all* areas of our lives and 2) knowing that whatever material wealth we possess actually belongs to our Father.

We are prosperous, healthy, and wealthy *because our Father owns it all*, and He gives it to us according to our faith. *Prosperity*, as we will see in our study in this book, means having your needs met and enough more to help others and give into the Lord's work.

The key is whether or not material possessions have you instead of you having them.

If you do have great material possessions, could you give them away if your Father said to do so?

If they were destroyed somehow, could you walk away trusting your Father to provide again?

If you cannot answer yes to both those questions, then you need to realize you may have an "idol" in your life, something that is more important to you than God. Certainly, your attitude is not Christ-like, as we will see in our study.

An old saying sort of puts the way we ought to see money into perspective: "Money will buy a fine dog, but only love will make him wag his tail."

Another saying looks at prosperity from the other angle: "I've been poor, and I've been rich — and rich is better!"

Put those two together, and you have a closer idea of God's intention for His children: financial prosperity governed by love of God (which implies obedience to Him) and compassion for one's fellowman.

The principles in this book are not theoretical but literal and practical. They have worked in my own life. I have seen them work in the lives of my friends and associates throughout this country and, in fact, around the world. I have seen them work in churches and in the lives of many members of my church.

They have worked for millions of people, and they will work for you — the reader of this book. God has no favorites. What He does for one child, He will do for another. God is no respecter of persons. (Acts 10:34.) Our inheritance already has been provided. Our part is to mature in the faith in order to know how to receive on earth what is possible to receive here.

We must do our part, and our part involves a lot of study and meditation and hard work. (2 Tim. 2:15.)

One of the greatest ways I have found to study God's Word is to rise early every morning and read two chapters in the Old Testament, five chapters in Psalms, one in Proverbs, and two in the New Testament. When you complete each section, start over. This will get you through the Old Testament once each year, Psalms and Proverbs each month, and the New Testament twice each year.

I urge you to approach this book with this attitude: "I have to see the answer in Scripture before I believe it."

Every point I make in this book is backed up by Scripture, and I do not mean a few verses used as a "jumping-off point" for my pet theories. Instead, you will find this book actually saturated with dozens of verses out of which my explanations flow (*exegesis*). "Theories" are not important. What God said is what is important!

My only function is to explain and correlate the various verses of scripture. You can place your faith in these financial principles. If we cannot believe God's promises in the area of finances, how can we believe His promises for eternal salvation?

If we can believe *some* of what God's Word says, we should be able to believe *all* that is in the Bible!

My greatest desire in life is to communicate the teachings of God's Word to other people. Join with me and let us study exactly what Scripture teaches about trusting God for success and finances.

1
Should Christians Prosper?

... The Lord be exalted, who delights in the well-being (prosperity) of his servant.

Psalm 35:27 NIV

Have you ever asked yourself any of the following questions?

• Does God really want me to be successful and financially prosperous?

• Does the Bible not say that money is the root of all evil?

• Does God really care about my success and financial condition?

• Does God care if I drive an old car and live in a rundown apartment or if I drive a Mercedes and live in a $200,000 home?

• Will I not prosper as much if I just work hard?

• Does the Bible teach us to get out of debt?

• Is tithing for today?

• How can I possibly increase my giving, if I cannot even pay my bills with the money I now earn?

• Is it wrong for Christians to have substantial amounts of money in bank accounts and investments?

9

• Are there definite scriptures I can get in agreement with to enjoy His blessings everywhere I turn?

• Were the blessings found in Deuteronomy 18 just for the Israelites? Or are they for Christians today as well?

Each of those questions and other similar questions will be answered in this book. The way to prosper and be successful is by following God's laws of success and prosperity outlined in His Word. If we follow these laws exactly, we will prosper exactly the way God want us to prosper. There is absolutely nothing wrong with the biblical kind of success and prosperity.

Many Christians believe that *money is the root of all evil.* This is incorrect. Money in itself is not evil:

Money builds churches.

Money sends missionaries all over the world.

Money produces Christian radio and television programs.

Money produces Christian books and cassette tapes. No, money is not evil.

What the Bible really says is the *love of money* is "the root of all evil."

The Bible tells us there is a way to prosper that is not evil, and it is by following God's laws of success and prosperity. When this is done, we will prosper in every way, not just financially.

God created all the wealth of this earth. Did He create it for unbelievers — hard-hearted sinful men and women who curse Him, deny Him, and disobey His laws? Does He really want them to prosper and His children to do without? This idea does not make any sense at all.

God is a more loving Father than any earthly father. He wants the best for His children. He does not want us to be financial failures in any way. Just as children in the world are a reflection of their parents, Christians should be a reflection of our Parent.

He wants the world to see successful and prosperous, joyful, loving Christians. If our Father gave us His only Son, why then would He hold anything else back from us? Already, He has given us His best. Does it make any sense to believe He would refuse to give us the rest?

He that spared not His own Son, but delivered him up for us all, how shall he not with him also freely give all things?

Romans 8:32

How can we, therefore, accept one promise — salvation — and deny other promises such as healing or success and prosperity?

David's most well-known psalm, **The Lord is my shepherd; I shall not want** (Ps. 23:1), conceived in the mind of the Lord and inspired by the Holy Spirit, expresses God's concern and diligent care for those who follow Him.

We are the cherished objects of His divine love. He cares for each of us as a Father cares for His children and as a Shepherd for His sheep.

God Wants His Best for Us

Two truths are emphasized in the 23rd Psalm:

1. God through Christ and by the Holy Spirit is so concerned about each of His children He desires to love, care for, protect, guide, and be near us. We are the special objects of His affection and attention.

11

2. The Lord has redeemed us with His shed blood, and we now belong to Him. As His children, we can claim the promises of His Word.

I shall not be in want means I will not lack anything necessary for my wellbeing. I will be content in good times and bad times, because I trust in His love and His commitment to me: **. . . Those who seek the Lord lack no good thing** (Ps. 34:10 NIV).

God will supply our needs, give us abundant life, hear our prayers, comfort us with His presence, and redeem us — but only if we seek Him. We must cry out to Him, draw close to Him, and remain free from sin, so that God can bless us as children.

It is normally God's will that believers be healthy and that our lives be accompanied by His blessings. He wants all to go well with us (i.e. that our works, plans, purposes, families go according to His will and direction for our lives).

It is God's will that we be successful and prosperous.

It is God's will that we earn enough to provide shelter, food, and clothing for ourselves and our families, and have enough to help others and to further Christ's cause.

We know God is able to supply our needs, and that He promised to supply us according to His glorious riches in Christ Jesus. If Philippians 4:19 were the only verse we had concerning how God feels about our success and prosperity, it would be enough. There are, however, dozens more, such as John 10:10 where Jesus said: **. . . I am come that they might have life, and that they might have it more abundantly**.

It seems to me logic alone would tell us it is God's will for us to be successful and to prosper and be healthy.

Ask yourself these questions:

12

Will God violate His own Word?

Will God break His covenant with us?

The answers to these questions are, "Of course not!"

Insecurities are real, but dwell on the good and positive. You must overcome all your insecurities. If you obey God's Word, it will bring blessing on your life. Stand true to Jesus. Hebrews 4:12,13 NIV says:

> **For the Word of God is living and active. Sharper than any double-edged sword, it penetrates even to dividing soul and spirit, joints and marrow; it judges the thoughts and attitudes of the heart.**

Nothing in all creation is hidden from God's sight. Everything is uncovered and laid bare before the eyes of Him to whom we must some day give an account of our lives. Many great men of God have prospered and been successful as a result of following God's laws for success and prosperity.

One good example of the application of these laws can be seen in the life of Abraham. Abraham lived a very fruitful prosperous life: **And Abram was very rich in cattle, in silver, and in gold** (Gen. 13:2).

The New Testament clearly teaches that, because of the price paid by Jesus Christ, all Christians are heirs to the same blessings that Abraham received from God. (Gal. 3:14.)

> **And if ye be Christ's, then are ye Abraham's seed, and heirs according to the promise.**
>
> **Galatians 3:29**

God's Word clearly tells us that we are heirs to Abraham. This means the blessings God gave Abraham are available to us. Our Father wants us to receive those blessings. We can receive them by following His laws of success and prosperity.

If someone says God does not want us to prosper materially, how can they possibly explain the following verse?

But thou shalt remember the Lord thy God: for it is he that giveth thee power to get wealth, that he may establish his covenant which he sware unto thy fathers, as it is this day.

Deuteronomy 8:18

If it is wrong to be successful and prosperous, why does God give us the power to become wealthy as part of His covenant?

It is true that many people have been destroyed by wealth, because they did not obtain it or did not maintain it through following God's laws. However, that does not mean prosperity was evil, only that their attitude toward it was wrong.

There is absolutely nothing wrong with being prosperous and successful *if* we obtain and retain our prosperity as a result of following God's laws.

2
Prosperous Men and Women of the Bible

... Blessed is the man that feareth the Lord, that delighteth greatly in His commandments. His seed shall be mighty upon earth: the generation of the upright shall be blessed. Wealth and riches shall be in his house: and his righteousness endureth for ever.

Psalms 112:1-3

If prosperity is wrong, God certainly would not have inspired the psalmist to write that wealth and riches will be in our homes if we fear Him (hold Him in respect and awe) and if we follow His laws.

How can someone believe it is wrong to be successful and prosperous and explain why many of the greatest biblical men of God were prosperous and successful?

If it is wrong to be materially prosperous, then Abraham, Isaac, Jacob, Joseph, David, Solomon — and I could name many more — were living in sin and out of the will of God!

We usually hear Job mentioned in terms of God's "teaching someone a lesson through poverty," as if Job's wealth was wrong and the cause of his trouble. However, if you read the book of Job carefully, you can see *the devil* destroyed Job's wealth. The "hole" in Job's life that caused God to allow this was *fear*. (Job 3:25.)

In fact, after his trying and testing was over, God gave Job twice as much wealth as he had lost — 14,000 sheep, 6,000 camels, 1,000 teams of oxen, 1,000 female donkeys, many servants, and a great house. (Job 42:12.)

He also gave him more sons and daughters, which the Bible counts among a man's "wealth." (Ps. 127:5.) Today's "killing fields" of abortion clinics are robbing America of its greatest wealth: a large percentage of its future generations.

At least two of Jesus' followers were rich men: Joseph of Arimathea (Matt. 27:57) and Nicodemus, a member of the Sanhedrin, the Jewish ruling council. (John 3.) There is absolutely nothing wrong with financial prosperity unless it comes ahead of God.

Our Father wants us to have money, but He does not want money to have us! Let us look at a few initial verses of scripture to help us understand the character of God, from which we can begin to know His ways.

> **God is not a man, that he should lie; neither the son of man, that he should repent: hath he said, and shall he not do it? or hath He spoken, and shall he not make it good?**
>
> **Numbers 23:19**

> **There shall not any man be able to stand before thee all the days of thy life: as I was with Moses, so I will be with thee: I will not fail thee, nor forsake thee.**
>
> **Joshua 1:5**

The grass withereth, the flower fadeth: but the word of our God shall stand for ever.

Isaiah 40:8

In order to obtain anything from God, we must ask in faith. (Heb. 11:6.) To raise our level of faith to obtain, it is important to know that God is love (1 John 4:8,16) and that He is a giving God. (John 3:16; Rom. 8:32.) God gave us His precious promises so we can be like He is, if we follow them.

Whereby are given unto us exceeding great and precious promises: that by these ye might be partakers of the divine nature, having escaped the corruption that is in the world through lust.

2 Peter 1:4

Prosperity and abundance are part of God's divine nature. He owns the whole world and everything in the world. He has given us more than 3,000 promises in His Word so that, by these promises, we can partake of His divine nature.

God Is Prosperous, and We Are in His Image

The very first chapter of the Bible says: **And God said, Let us make man in our image, after our likeness . . .** (Gen. 1:26). If the Godhead (Father, Son, and Holy Spirit) is prosperous and created us to be like He is, is it not obvious He wants us to prosper also?

The more we study God's Word, the more evidence we see of His plans for our abundance and prosperity. God created great abundance when he created the earth.

Then God said, "Let the waters teem with fish and other life, and let the skies be filled with birds of every kind." So God created great sea creatures, and every sort of fish and every kind of bird. And God looked at them with pleasure, and blessed them all.

"Multiply and stock the oceans," he told them, and to the birds he said, "Let your numbers increase. Fill the earth!"

Genesis 1:20-22 TLB

We can see further signs of the abundance our Father planned for us by looking inside a watermelon, an apple, an orange, a grapefruit, and many other fruits and vegetables. Our Father provided us with seeds to reproduce what we use many times over.

And he said, "Let the earth burst forth with every sort of grass and seedbearing plant, and fruit trees with seeds inside the fruit, so that these seeds will produce the kinds of plants and fruit they came from." And so it was, and God was pleased.

Genesis 1:11 TLB

The first chapter of Genesis tells us how God stocked the earth with fish, animals, and birds and how He provided plants and fruit trees. When God finished doing this, He then created a man who was meant to enjoy this abundance and to be master (have dominion) over the earth and everything on the earth.

Then God said, "Let us make a man — someone like ourselves, to be the master of all life upon the earth and in the skies and in the seas."

Genesis 1:26 TLB

That man was our forefather, Adam. God provided Adam with great abundance. He had everything he could ever want. However, Adam forfeited his riches and his dominion (stewardship and administration) to Satan. Adam forfeited the abundance and prosperity God intended for His children. This brings us to the reason why God sent His Son, Jesus Christ, to earth.

18

Again and again I have asked Bible school students for the precise reason that Jesus Christ was sent to this earth. Only a very small percentage knew the correct answer. Do you?

Jesus was sent here for one purpose: *to destroy the works of Satan*, the arch enemy of the Godhead and His children. Man's salvation is simply the result of the destruction of Satan's works: **. . . For this purpose the Son of God was manifested, that he might destroy the works of the devil** (1 John 3:8).

Jesus succeeded in His mission. This is why, just before ascending into heaven, He said, **All power is given unto me in heaven and in earth** (Matt. 28:18).

Before He ascended to the right hand of the Father, He delegated the authority of His name to His Body — His "hands and feet" on earth. (Matt. 18:18; Luke 10:19,20; Eph. 4:15,16; 1 Cor. 12:12-27.)

Jesus won back every bit of power and authority Satan had usurped from Adam. He restored our abundance. Jesus paid the full price so His brothers and sisters could prosper.

> **For ye know the grace of our Lord Jesus Christ, that, though he was rich, yet for your sakes he became poor, that ye through his poverty might be rich.**
>
> **2 Corinthians 8:9**

Some Christians believe this verse of scripture does not refer to financial riches. They say God is talking only about spiritual riches. I do not agree *because of the context of that verse.*

Paul Wrote Much About Finances

Anyone who reads 2 Corinthians 8 and 9 at one time can see both chapters deal primarily with *finances.* Because *The Living Bible Paraphrased* is easy to understand, let us refer to several verses of scripture before and after 2 Corinthians 8:9 in that version to be sure we do have the subject in its right context.

> **Though they have been going through much trouble and hard times, they have mixed their wonderful joy with their deep poverty, and the result has been an overflow of giving to others. They gave not only what they could afford, but far more; and I can testify that they did it because they wanted to, and not because of nagging on my part. They begged us to take the money so they could share in the joy of helping the Christians in Jerusalem** (vv. 2-4).

Verse 2 speaks about the deep poverty, trouble, and hard times being experienced by the churches of Macedonia. Verses 3 and 4 tell us they gave more money than they could afford to give.

> **Having started the ball rolling so enthusiastically, you should carry this project through to completion just as gladly, giving whatever you can out of whatever you have. . . . If you are really eager to give, then it isn't important how much you have to give. God wants you to give what you have, not what you haven't** (vv. 11,12).

Verse 11 speaks of finishing a project by giving whatever you can out of whatever you have. Verse 12 again refers to the importance of giving. Chapter 9 talks in detail about giving to the poor and about the abundance God will give us in return.

There is no question that Chapters 8 and 9 of 2 Corinthians deal primarily with the subject of finances, or that verse 8 — which tells us Jesus became poor so that we could become rich — is right in the middle of Paul's discourse on finances.

Some Christians use 2 Corinthians 8:9 to "prove" that Jesus Christ was poor during His earthly ministry. They say His life was a model for our lives; therefore, we are not meant to prosper, especially those in the ministry. As we examine the gospels carefully, many readers will be surprised to see that Jesus was not poor when He walked on the earth 2,000 years ago.

3
Was Jesus Really Poor?

The earth is the Lord's, and the fulness thereof, the world, and they that dwell therein (Ps. 24:1) **. . . . Though He was rich, yet for your sakes He *became* poor, that ye through His poverty might be rich** (2 Cor. 8:9).

Do those verses tell us clearly from both the Old and New Testaments that Jesus was *financially* poor during His earthly ministry? No, David wrote that God (Father, Son, Holy Spirit) owns everything, and Paul wrote that Jesus *became* poor.

When did Jesus "become" poor? I believe Jesus became poor when He made the supreme sacrifice on the cross at Calvary. Jesus gave up everything at that time — even His clothing.

In spite of many pictures to the contrary, Jesus was completely naked when He died on the cross. He could not have been any poorer than He was at that time. When He died, He did not own one thing in this world. While He hung on the cross, Roman soldiers gambled for the clothing He had worn.

Yes, Jesus became poor, but study the four gospels which tell us about His life to see if he really lived in poverty. Jesus' family may not have been wealthy while He was growing up as

23

the son of a carpenter; however, remember the gifts of the magi who came to see Him in Bethlehem? (Luke 2:11.)

Gold, frankincense, and myrrh were very expensive gifts, valued at a lot of money! In traditional religious thinking, preachers and teachers almost totally ignore the monetary value and talk about the symbolical meaning of those gifts.

Yet the gifts were not just "symbols," but literal, valuable items. What happened to them? We are not told. However, knowing God as a loving heavenly Father, it is reasonable to suppose He sent those things for Joseph to be able to take care of Mary and Jesus.

Carpenters in those days did not just nail boards together. They were woodsmen, craftsmen, contractors, and furniture makers. They had to be healthy enough to go out and fell trees and work them up into lumber with primitive tools. (In Jesus' day, Judea, Galilee, and the surrounding areas were still heavily wooded.)

The Bible Almanac says carpenters were usually "talented wood carvers."[1] They built houses, crafted fine furniture and carved fancy doors, and so forth. If Joseph turned the Magi's gifts into finances in Egypt, do you think he returned to Nazareth a pauper? I expect he went home with enough to set up a fine shop. I seriously doubt if his family ever lacked for food or clothing.

However, we are not told anything of those years, so we can only make some inferences from the fact that the baby Jesus was given some valuable gifts that do not show up in His ministry years. The only logical assumption is that they were used to give them a start in Egypt.

We *can* get an idea of the prosperity of Jesus' earthly ministry — the approximate three-year period between the time

He was baptized and filled with God's Holy Spirit in the Jordan River and the time He was crucified on the cross.

Was Jesus a "Poor" Evangelist?

Was He really poor during this great three-year period which changed the earth forever? Let us examine the facts. Some people believe that Jesus was poor because He said:

... Foxes have holes, and birds of the air have nests; but the Son of man hath not where to lay his head.

Luke 9:58

Jesus apparently did not own a personal home where He spent every night, because He was the first traveling evangelist. Also, for years a number of so-called "prophets" and zealots (leaders of rebel bands against Roman rule) also had roamed the countryside — to say nothing of John the Baptist. All slept in the fields or caves as they traveled.

Jesus was constantly on the move, but surely He could have stayed in the home of the wealthy Joseph of Arimathea (Matt. 27:57) or in other nice homes where He would have been welcomed. In fact, we will see shortly that Jesus could have produced the money to stay each night in an inn if He had so chosen. Also, He may have rented a headquarters house in Capernaum to which He returned periodically. Matthew 4:13 says He "moved to" (dwelt in) Capernaum, not Nazareth.

In Mark 2:1, He returned to Capernaum from a ministry trip and **it was noised that he was in the house**. What house? Was it a rented house? Or perhaps it was Peter's house? The writers of the gospels refer to "the house" as if it were common knowledge where He lived.

On His travels around the countryside, I believe He slept in the open air by choice and not by necessity, because it was the way travelers then had to do. In fact, the "inn" where Mary and Joseph tried to find a place is the word *khan*, a "cara-vanserai," not a hotel as inns are today.

These *caravanserai* mostly catered to travelers in caravans, and Bethlehem was the "jumping off" point for caravans to Egypt. Most of those staying there only rented space in an open courtyard.[2] What with the noise of animals and people, and the smoke from a number of campfires, to say nothing of the smells, God blessed Mary and Joseph with privacy and quiet in a cave.

We usually think of Jesus as being born to such a poor family that His birth was in "a lowly stable." Actually, "prosperity" in this case *was* a stable where curious onlookers could not see or hear Mary giving birth. Jesus had a manger to sleep in — warm and cozy, protected from the night air, smoky campfires, and strong smells of the "inn."

When He began evangelizing, is it not a fact that 12 disciples, and at times, 70 other men, traveled with Him, to say nothing of other followers who are mentioned from time to time?

Were the needs of all of these people and their families not met?

How can anyone say that Jesus was poor, if He was able to meet the needs of such a large group of people?

How many poor people run an organization of this size?

How many poor people have a treasurer to keep track of their finances? Jesus and His organization had a treasurer. Judas was their "treasurer." (John 13:29.)

Furthermore, would a "poor man" be able to feed large groups of 4,000 to 5,000 men and their families?

Jesus was a complete master of God's laws of prosperity, *because He knew and understood the Father*. He used those laws repeatedly to meet His needs.

26

"What about the 5,000 men I fed with five loaves of bread? How many basketfuls of scraps did you pick up afterwards?"

"Twelve," they said.

"And when I fed the 4,000 with seven loaves, how much was left?"

"Seven basketfuls," they said.

"And yet you think I'm worried that we have no bread?"

Mark 8:19-21 TLB

What poor man could provide for others like this? When the tax collectors of Capernaum came to Peter and asked for money, was Jesus able to pay them? He certainly was.

Here is what He said to Peter, "Go down to the shore and throw in a line, and in the mouth of the first fish that bites, you will find money for your taxes and mine. Go and pay them." (Matt. 17:27.)

Jesus Lived by God's Laws

Jesus obviously was able to master laws of prosperity in order to pay His taxes and Peter's taxes. He could have used these same laws to produce money for any of His other needs, if He so chose. When Peter and the other disciples had fished all night and had come up empty, Jesus was able to produce so many fish that the nets broke. (Luke 5:1-11.)

A similar instance is reported in John 21:1-11. When Jesus needed a donkey to ride into Jerusalem on that first Palm Sunday, He did not have to rent or buy one. He simply sent two disciples to the village of Bethphage to find a donkey and its colt tied alongside the road. He told them to take these animals and, if anyone questioned them, to say that "the Lord needed them." This is exactly what happened. (Matt. 21:1-7.)

When Jesus needed a room to serve the Passover meal, He did not go to a hotel to rent one. Instead, He sent two disciples into Jerusalem and told them to contact a certain man who would lead them to another man. They should tell the second man they needed a large upper room, and he would take care of everything. That is exactly what happened. (Mark 14:12-16.)

How can anyone claim that Jesus was poor when He was able to obtain transportation and hotel rooms so easily?

When Jesus hung on the cross, the soldiers who crucified Him gambled for possession of His expensive, seamless, one-piece robe. If He was poor during His earthly ministry, where did He get a robe so valuable that soldiers gambled for it?

You might wonder what connection there is between the miracles performed by Jesus and His financial prosperity. The answer is that Jesus Christ had the purest faith ever seen on earth. As a result, He was able to turn little into plenty. He had no need for worldly, material assets, because He knew He could apply His faith to God's laws of prosperity in order to obtain whatever He needed.

Perhaps you are thinking, "Yes, but He is the Son of God. What does this have to do with me? I cannot use God's laws of prosperity and success to provide miracles like Jesus did."

Jesus clearly told us that He did not perform any of His miracles with His own ability, and He said we could do the same works and more:

> . . . **Verily, verily, I say unto you, The Son can do nothing of himself** (John 5:19). . . . **I can of mine own self do nothing** (John 5:30). . . . **but the Father that dwelleth in me, he doeth the works** (John 14:10).
>
> **Verily, verily, I say unto you, He that believeth on me, the works that I do shall he do also; and greater works than these shall he do; because I go unto my Father.**

And whatsoever ye shall ask in my name, that will I do, that the Father may be glorified in the Son. If you shall ask any thing in my name, I will do it.

John 14:12-14

On earth, He limited Himself to His human abilities. In other words, He had to live out His life as a man, not as God. He was able to perform these miracles only because He yielded completely to the Holy Spirit who lived inside of Him, not because He used any of His divine powers on earth.

You and I can do great works also here on earth — financially and otherwise — because Jesus defeated Satan and his works on the cross and delegated His authority to us. (John 14:12-14.) In addition, God's Word clearly tells us we have the *same* Holy Spirit living inside of us: **. . . The Spirit of Him who raised up Jesus from the dead dwells in you** (Rom. 8:11 Amp).

Jesus Christ followed God's laws of prosperity, as well as all of God's other laws. He did not rely in the least on His own ability. He relied totally upon God's Word and upon God's Holy Spirit living within Him. Because Jesus followed all of God's laws of prosperity, He enjoyed total prosperity — not just financial prosperity — but total prosperity of the spirit, soul and body — throughout His earthly ministry.

We Can Live by the Same Laws

John 14:12-14 tells us we can enjoy this same total prosperity during our lives here on earth. There is no question about it. Our Father wants His children to prosper and be in health instead of the evil sinners who now enjoy much of the world's prosperity.

"The evil man may accumulate money like dust, with closets jammed full of clothing — yes he may order

29

**them made by his tailor, but the innocent shall wear
that clothing, and shall divide his silver among them."**

Job 27:16,17 TLB

Yes, our Father wants us to prosper financially. However,
this prosperity is not automatic any more than salvation is
automatic. All of God's provisions for us must be *received by
faith*. Simply because we become born again, we are not
automatically healed. Healing is provided in the atonement,
yet we have to receive it by faith.

We also have to follow His laws of prosperity, which I have
carefully laid out in this book. If we follow these laws, God will
not withhold any good thing from us. (Ps. 84:11.) Each day He
loads us down with benefits. (Ps. 68:19.)

God's promise of blessings to Israel through the blood
covenant with Abraham also have come on us, as children
of Abraham through Jesus and the New blood covenant.
(Gal. 3:29.)

Deuteronomy 28:1-15 (NIV) spells out the promises for us:

**If you fully obey the Lord your God and carefully
follow all his commands I give you today, the Lord
your God will set you high above all the nations on
earth. All these blessings will come upon you and
accompany you if you obey the Lord your God. You
will be blessed in the city and blessed in the country.
... You will be blessed when you come in and blessed
when you go out.... The Lord will send a blessing on
your barns and on everything you put your hands to.
... The Lord will grant you abundant prosperity....
The Lord will open the heavens, the storehouse of
His bounty, to send rain on your land in season and
to bless all the work of your hands. ... If you pay
attention to the commands I give you this day and
carefully follow them, you will always be at the top,**

never at the bottom. Do not turn aside from any of the commands I give you today, to the right or to the left, following other gods and serving them.

[1] Packer, J.I., Tenney, Merrill C., White, William Jr. *The Bible Almanac*, (Nashville: Thomas Nelson Publishers, 1980), p. 273.

[2] Wight, Fred H. *Manners and Customs of Bible Lands*, (Chicago: Moody Press, 1953, 1983), pp. 272-274; *Jesus and His Times*, (Pleasantville, N.Y.: Reader's Digest Association, Inc.), p. 20.

4
Don't Be a "Hyper-Faith" Christian

... Let the Lord be magnified, which hath pleasure in the prosperity of His servant.

Psalm 35:27

In the Introduction, I talked of two positions Christians have taken on the subject of financial prosperity and success. The first two chapters have been spent discussing why our Father *does* want us to prosper financially and those who equate spirituality and poverty are not biblically correct.

Before moving on to God's laws and how to use them, let us look at the other extreme: the "hyper-faith" Christian who measures spirituality by prosperity.

This person says, "Of course God wants me to prosper! I'm going to follow His laws of prosperity and get myself a Rolls Royce, a $500,000 home, and a million dollars."

That is not God's way, but the way carnal, worldly people approach the subject of prosperity. They put their selfish desires first. There is nothing wrong with owning a nice car and nice home, but possessions must never in any way preempt God.

I have spent hundred of hours studying what the Bible has to say about financial prosperity. If I had to boil everything

33

I have learned down to just four words, this "prescription" for God's prosperity and success would be *always keep God first*. Jesus said the same thing differently.

Seek ye first the kingdom of God, and his right-eousness; and all these things will be added unto you.
Matthew 6:33

Whatever any of us needs in any area of our lives, God's laws say He will provide them to the exact degree that we keep Him first in every area of our lives.

Exactly what does it mean to always keep God first? One example is never to start a day without a period of quiet time of prayer and devotion. Another example is to set definite goals of Bible study and meditation and to consistently reach these goals, because they are put ahead of family time, watching television, and enjoying hobbies.

Many Christians believe they always keep God first, but if they were completely honest, they would have to admit that really, they only give God some time Sunday mornings, perhaps at one or two Christian meetings each week, and for a few minutes of prayer daily. This lifestyle obviously does not put God first.

Many of us have accepted Jesus as Savior, but we have never truly allowed Jesus to be Lord over every area of our lives. In order to put Jesus first, we need to deny our own desires and wants in favor of doing His will.

. . . If any man will come after me, let him deny himself, and take up his cross daily, and follow me.
Luke 9:23

Accepting Jesus as Lord and Savior demands not only believing the truth of the gospel, but also committing ourselves to follow him.

Money Cannot Buy Happiness or Eternal Life

The world's system of prosperity and success puts other things ahead of God or in place of God — money, success, possessions, and ego recognition.

That entire worldview is in violation of God's laws of prosperity and success. Our Father wants us to prosper financially, but only if prosperity and the things it will buy never in any way come ahead of Him.

In order to illustrate this point, look at the goals of a typical, ambitious, worldly young man as he graduates from college and steps out into the world. Would you agree that many ambitious young people are seeking fame and fortune and a long life?

God's Word tells us exactly how to achieve these goals — through true humility and respect for Him. (Prov. 22:4.) Once again we see there is not anything wrong with riches, provided they are obtained God's way.

What is God's way for obtaining riches, honor, and a long life? His Word says we obtain these things by constantly humbling ourselves before our awesome respect for Him. This is God's "prescription" for prosperity and success in every area of our lives: *Surrender your lives totally to Me.* Put Him in complete charge of everything there is. (Heb. 2:8.)

He does not want us to put family, money, hobbies, or anything else ahead of Him: **Thou shalt have no other gods before me** (Ex. 20:3). This command prohibited the polytheism that characterized all the religions of the ancients. Today, we may not have many obvious "gods," but anything that comes before God in our lives has become an idol.

Believers' worship must be directed to God alone. There may be no worshipping, praying to, or seeking guidance and

35

help from, any other gods, any spirits, or the dead. The world's system of prosperity and success puts money and the things it can buy ahead of God.

In fact, many people get so caught up with earning money they think about it constantly. The love of money is the center of their lives. It consumes them. It drives them constantly. Money has become their "god."

If they are not thinking about making money, they are thinking about how to invest it or what they can buy with it. Money takes first place in their lives. They cannot get enough of it. The more they get, the more they want.

This all-consuming desire for money is exactly the kind of desire we should have for God. We should think about Him all the time. He should be at the very center of our existence. Every aspect of our lives should revolve around Him. We should not ever be able to get enough of Him. The more we learn of God and His ways, the more we should want to learn. This is the way to prosperity and success.

We will never want for anything as long as we constantly put the Lord first and keep Him first. Those who seek the Lord shall not want any good thing. (Ps. 34:10). The world searches eagerly for wealth and recognition from other people, but these things truly only come from God. When we are in right standing with Him, when we love Him more than anything else and always keep Him first, we will receive all the riches and honor we will ever want or need.

> **I love them that love me; and those that seek me early shall find me. Riches and honour are with me; yea, durable riches and righteousness.**
>
> **Proverbs 8:17,18**

Many of us have fallen into the trap of not keeping God first. In fact, many of us allow the problems in our lives to take predominance over God.

Too many of us think, "I need this. I have to have that, and I do not know how to solve this problem."

Instead, we should say. "God, I'm going to put you first and keep you first every hour of every day of my life. I'm going to study and meditate constantly in Your Word and do exactly what it tells me to do, trusting completely in you to supply every one of my needs."

Are You Problem-Centered or God-Centered?

Too many Christians (often without even realizing it) are much more problem-centered than they are God-centered. We spend too much time focusing on our problems and too little time focusing on Almighty God and His ability to solve every problem to the exact degree we can let go and trust Him to solve them.

If God really is first in our lives, why should we ever be worried about any problem?

If we are worried about any problem, are we not allowing that problem to take first place ahead of God? Instead of constantly focusing on the problem, we should focus constantly on the great promises of God's Word and the great ability of God's Holy Spirit living inside of us.

Thou wilt keep him in perfect peace, whose mind is stayed on thee: because he trusteth in thee.

Isaiah 26:3

God will keep in perfect peace the remnant who remain steadfast and faithful to their Lord. In times of trouble, we must continually strive to keep our minds turned to the Lord in prayer, trust, and hope. We must place our trust in Him because He is a rock who endures forever.

He is a sure and firm foundation. A peace is available to us that is perfect — a total, complete, and absolute peace! Perfect peace certainly includes financial prosperity.

How can we have that peace if we worry about financial problems? God's requirements for perfect peace are very clear:

Firstly, we must keep Him first at all times. We must keep our minds focused on Him at all times and not on our problems.

Secondly, we must trust Him completely. We must pay the price to find out what His Word says He will do and then believe He will do what He says.

God's laws of prosperity only work to the degree that we keep Him first in our lives — totally, completely, and absolutely ahead of everything else. They are based on total dedication of our lives to Him. Our blessings will be in direct proportion to the degree of true, deep, and lasting commitment to Him.

Money "talks," but we ought not to listen to money, but to God. A man named Ray O. Jones gave us the right perspective, when he said, "Listen to this dollar speak":

"You hold me in your hand and call me yours. Yet may I not as well call you mine? See how easily I rule you? To gain me, you would all but die. I am invaluable as rain, essential as water. Without me, men and institutions would die. Yet I do not hold the power of life for them: I am futile *without the stamp of your desire.*

"I go nowhere unless you send me. I keep strange company. For me, men mock, love, and scorn character. Yet, I am appointed to the service of saints, to give education to the growing mind and food to the starving bodies of the poor. My power is terrific.

Handle me carefully and wisely, lest you become my servant rather than I yours."[1]

[1]Tan, Paul Lee. *Encyclopedia of 7700 Illustrations*, (Rockville, MD: Assurance Publishers, 1979), p. 823, #3524.

5
No Human Being Really "Owns" Anything

Beloved, I wish above all things that thou mayest prosper and be in health, even as thy soul prospereth.

3 John 2

God's laws of prosperity and success are founded upon the fact that *He owns everything and we own nothing*. Do you think you own your car? Your home? And the other possessions which, according to man's laws, you own?

God's ways are usually quite different from man's ways, and this is a specific example. God's Word clearly tells us that we do not own anything. When you grasp the truth that God just lets us use His things, then His laws of prosperity and success start to fall into place.

We came into this world empty-handed, and we will leave this world the same way: **For we brought nothing into this world, and it is certain we can carry nothing out** (1 Tim. 6:7). While we are here, God allows us to make use of possessions that actually belong to Him.

Behold, the heaven and the heaven of heavens is the Lord's thy God, the earth also, with all that therein is.

Deuteronomy 10:14

Every bit of money on this earth is owned by God, not by us: **The silver is mine, and the gold is mine, saith the Lord of hosts** (Haggai 2:8). God owns everything in Heaven, everything on earth, and everything in between. He owns the sun, moon, stars, and all the planets of the universe. Our money belongs to God. All the things we think we own belong to God. We ourselves belong to God. (1 Cor. 6:20, 7:23.)

The earth is the Lord's and the fulness thereof; the world, and they that dwell therein.

Psalm 24:1

Some people read these statements and think, "My possessions belong to me. I earned them. I worked hard to get them. I can do what I want with them."

God's Word says:

And thou shalt say in thine heart, My power and the might of mine hands hath gotten me this wealth. But thou shalt remember the Lord thy God: for it is he that giveth thee power to get wealth. . .

Deuteronomy 8:17,18

This verse affirms that God blessed His people as a sign he was honoring the covenant with Abraham and His descendants. Most people who become wealthy following the world's system of prosperity and success do not understand this concept. This is why God's Word says it is so difficult for most wealthy people to enter into God's kingdom.

. . . Children, how hard is it for them that trust in riches to enter into the kingdom of God! It is easier for a camel to go through the eye of a needle, than

42

for a rich man to enter into the kingdom of God.

Mark 10:24,25

The key words here are *trust in riches*. This is the world's way.

Is Heaven Closed to the Materially Wealthy?

God's laws of prosperity require us to trust in Him instead of trusting in riches. The world's way is to trust in material assets and to continually try to accumulate more of them. The more assets we have accumulated, the harder it is for us to enter into God's kingdom.

Was Jesus saying no person who has material wealth can ever go to Heaven? Of course not, yet that is the way some people read that story.

What Jesus was pointing out is that rich men tend to trust in their riches, which makes it difficult for them to love God more than money. God does not require every Christian to give away their money and possessions to get into Heaven, simply to give up *reliance on them* instead of Him.

It is interesting to note exactly what the phrase "eye of a needle" means. Some Bible scholars say "camel" should have been translated "rope," in the sense of a "rope being threaded through a needle. Others think Jesus was just using a funny analogy to point out the danger of trusting in riches.

Others say that many of the ancient cities of the Middle East were surrounded by high walls with large gates. When darkness came, these gates were closed so enemies could not attack the cities. However, a provision was made for late-arriving travelers to enter though a smaller gate.

That little door cut into one of the large gates could be opened so one man at a time could get into the city, but it was impossible for bands of men to rush through. Late-arriving travelers usually traveled on camels. The only way a camel could get through the door was by being completely unloaded of all of its goods and getting down on its knees to barely squeeze through.

Some scholars say there is no historical evidence for this.[1] However, it seems to me this is what Jesus was referring to in Mark 10:24. A rich man can enter God's kingdom, but it is not easy. Like a camel, he must completely unload all his worldly possessions (acknowledge God's ownership) and get down on his knees (surrender to Jesus and put Him first). Only then can the rich man enter into God's kingdom.

The world's system of prosperity and success is a full 180 degrees from this. In the world, millions think everything would be great if they only had unlimited funds. However, close observation of people who have more money than they can spend shows they do not find lasting satisfaction from wealth. It is foolish to think the world's prosperity and success can satisfy. The more we get the more we want.

He that loveth silver shall not be satisfied with silver; nor he that loveth abundance with increase: this is also vanity.

Ecclesiastes 5:10

Money and the abundance of material things do not give life meaning and thus cannot bring real happiness. Worldly possessions never satisfy. God did not create us that way. True satisfaction can only be found in Him deep within ourselves, not in any external worldly possessions.

Money Cannot Buy Happiness

Benjamin Franklin was a great thinker who once said:

Money never made a man happy yet, nor will it. There is nothing in its nature to produce happiness. The more a man

44

has, the more he wants. Instead of its filling a vacuum, it makes one. If it satisfies one want, it doubles and triples that want in other ways.[2]

The world's prosperity and success is empty. Most people who become rich without following God's laws of prosperity for success sooner or later think, "I have everything that I ever wanted and then some. How come I'm not happy and fulfilled? I feel so empty inside. Is this all there is to being wealthy?"

We see many people who have prospered by the world's system of prosperity who have family problems, divorce, spoiled children, adultery, and so forth. Others experience severe anxiety as they approach death and worry over estates which soon must be given up, perhaps to be fought over by selfish heirs and heiresses.

Solomon wrote: **The prosperity and success of fools shall destroy them** (Prov. 1:32). What is a fool? God's Word gives this definition of a fool: **The fool hath said in his heart, There is no God** (Ps. 53:1a).

Many financially successful people acknowledge God with their heads, but not with their hearts. Their hearts are caught up with making money and with the things it can buy. In reality money is their god. This is why man's methods of prosperity and success eventually destroy the people who follow them.

Prosperity and success apart from God bring trouble: **In the house of the righteous is much treasure: but in the revenues of the wicked is trouble** (Prov. 15:6). The world's system of prosperity has its price. It does not turn out the way men think it will.

Financial prosperity and success achieved by the world's methods will bring sorrow, but God's Word clearly teaches that His laws enable us to prosper in every area of our lives without any sorrow: **The blessing of the Lord, it maketh rich, and he addeth no sorrow with it** (Prov. 10:22).

All too often material wealth in this world is gained through wickedness and greed and is therefore not from God. True riches consist in the blessing of the Lord. Whether we are poor or rich, the Lord's presence and favor are our greatest wealth.

Where does sorrow come from? We have just seen that it does not come from following God's laws of prosperity and success.

> **For the love of money is the root of all evil: which while some coveted after, they have erred from the faith, and pierced themselves through with many sorrows.**
>
> **1 Timothy 6:10**

When we covet money and the things it will buy, we err from the faith, we go away from God, we move away from always putting Him first and trusting completely in Him. The love of money is not limited to the rich, however. Many people without much money still love it. They want it more than anything else and would do almost anything to obtain large amounts of it. These people are often tempted by get-rich-quick schemes.

God's Word says that get-rich-quick schemes are evil: **He that hasteth to be rich hath an evil eye . . .** (Prov. 28:22). In the Bible, we are warned over and over against coveting, against being greedy, and always wanting more. God hates covetousness: **. . . the covetous, whom the Lord abhorreth . . .** (Ps. 10:3). God wants us to hate covetousness, too. His Word says this right attitude will cause us to prolong our days: **. . . he that hateth covetousness shall prolong his days** (Prov. 28:16).

Our Father does not want our lives to center around money and the things money will buy. His Word tells us that the accumulation of money and possessions is not only wrong but will hurt us:

There is a sore evil which I have seen under the sun, namely riches kept for the owners thereof to their hurt.

Ecclesiastes 5:13

Money and the abundance of material things do not give life meaning and thus cannot bring real happiness. In general the honest working person who comes in after a good day's work sleeps peacefully, while wealthy individuals cannot sleep for fear that some calamity or a mistake will cause them to lose everything.

Even if they do not lose anything, they will take nothing with them when they die. It is sad that so many people work so hard for an abundance of possessions when it is much better to store up treasures in heaven.

Learn To Trust God

Millions of Christians have never really had to trust God for their finances, especially Christians in the middle and upper classes. Too many have lived a lifetime based upon worldly job security backed up by such things as a bank account, investments, equity in property, pension and profit-sharing plans, insurance, and so forth.

These things are not wrong, but they tend to insulate millions of Christians against learning and applying God's laws of prosperity and success. We must stop placing our trust in our various financial "cushions" and start trusting in God. God wants very much to supply all our needs during the difficult times which many economists believe are coming.

He will always do His part, but we must do our part. God's laws of prosperity and success will show us exactly how to profit during the coming economic crisis. (Isa. 48:17.)

No matter how bad our economy might get, God's laws of prosperity and success, if followed exactly, will provide us with financial substance that we need. If and when difficult economic times do come upon us, we will not solve our problems by "storing up" money and possessions.

If we hoard riches, we violate one of God's most important laws. The more we amass, the more we show our trust in what we have stored up instead of trusting in God. One example of this is the hoarding that always becomes prevalent in difficult times. During wars and crises, people hoard whatever is in short supply.

We saw this with sugar, gasoline, silk stockings, and other items in World War II. We saw another example of this in the gasoline shortages of 1973. Hoarding is always caused by fear, trusting in whatever is being stockpiled and not in God.

We are starting to see a lot of hoarding today as people anticipate the hard times that lie ahead. Some people are storing up large amounts of dehydrated food and canned goods. Others are storing up gold, silver, and precious gems in anticipation of a possible collapse of the world monetary system.

It concerns me to see many spiritual leaders advocating this. Some churches are selling "tribulation food." Some Christian leaders are advising us to convert everything we can to precious metals and gems. Is this spiritual?

This is the world's way of doing things! Hoarding is caused by fear and preoccupation with ourselves in opposition to the instructions in God's Word, which teach us to put God first, other people second, and ourselves last. God's ways are diametrically opposed to the world's ways. Instead of trusting in worldly riches, our Father clearly wants us to trust in Him and to share what we have with others.

Charge them that are rich in this world, that they be not high-minded, nor trust in uncertain riches, but in the living God, who giveth us richly all things to

enjoy; That they do good, that they be rich in good works, ready to distribute, willing to communicate.

1 Timothy 6:17-18

So far we have discussed primarily why God wants us to prosper and why God's ways differ from the world's ways. Now the time has come to switch our emphasis from *why* to *how* God wants us to prosper.

There is one step which must be taken before we make the transition from why to how. That is to renew our minds, to change our long-established thought processes from the world's methods of prosperity to God's laws of prosperity and success. Let us see what God's Word has to say about how we can do this.

[1] *Nelson's Illustrated Bible Dictionary*, (Nashville: Thomas Nelson Publishers, 1986), p. 365.

[2] Tan, *Encyclopedia of 7700 Illustrations*, p. 830, #3559.

6

Prosperity Means Conforming to God

. . . I am the Lord your God, which teacheth thee to profit, which leadeth thee by the way that thou shouldest go.

Isaiah 48:17

In order to be in a position for God to "teach us how to profit," we must stop conforming to the world's system of economics and finance, which is in complete contradiction to God's laws of prosperity and success. When we handle our finances exactly according to our Father's principles, our lives will be transformed.

Before our lives can be transformed, however, our *minds* must be transformed. How can we "transform" our minds? The Apostle Paul told us how in his epistle to the Christians at Rome, the center of world economics, culture, politics, and education in his time:

> **And be not conformed to this world: but be ye transformed by the *renewing* of your mind, that ye may prove what is that good, and acceptable, and perfect, will of God.**
>
> **Romans 12:2**

What does the word *renew* mean?

It means "to make new," or "to completely change." We must have our minds conformed to God's way of thinking by reading and meditating on His word. We must have our plans and ambitions determined by heavenly and eternal truths, not by this evil, temporal, and unstable age.

For example, when we see "urban renewal" being carried out in one of our cities, a portion of the city is totally altered, made brand new. This is what we must do with our minds before we can understand and apply God's laws of prosperity and success.

Our brains are the original computers, "the hardware," and still far ahead of anything man has been able to make as a copy. Our minds are the "software," so to speak, made up of all the information we have heard, read, and seen. Our minds must be "reprogrammed" to understand God's laws in any area.

Most of us need to feed a great deal of new data into our "computers." The only place to get the new "data" that replaces falsehoods with truth is from the Word of God.

Are you willing to replace the "programs" that have governed your lifetime financial habits in order to line up with God's laws instead of the world's system of finances?

If you are, God says this will transform your life. In fact, the Greek word *metamorphoo* (meaning "a metamorphosis," a complete change) used in Romans 12:2 is the very same word used in Matthew 17:2 and Mark 9:2 to describe the transfiguration, the complete change, of Jesus Christ.

This gives us some indication as to how greatly our lives can be transformed by the proper renewal of our minds. We will experience prosperity and health in exact proportion to the degree that our souls are prospered.

What is the *soul*? Our souls are our personalities, made up of our minds, our wills, and our emotions. In order to prosper, our souls must prosper, and our souls, in order to prosper, must be made brand new, reprogrammed with information from God's Word.

A prosperous soul is a soul filled with God's Word.

God wants us to constantly engage in the process of converting our souls from the world's ways to His ways. Even the most simple child could receive our Father's wisdom, if he were to know and follow God's principles.

> **The law of the Lord is perfect, converting the soul: the testimony of the Lord is sure, making wise the simple.**
>
> **Psalm 19:7**

Traditions, customs, the "way we have always done things" often nullifies the effectiveness of God's laws, Jesus said: **Making the Word of God of none effect through your tradition . . .** (Mark 7:13). As we constantly renew our thoughts, feelings, and emotions with God's Word, we will think, talk, and act more and more in line with the way our Father thinks, talks, and acts.

One evangelist tells of the time the Lord said to him, "If we are to continue to walk together in fellowship, one of us is going to have to change — and I never change!"

Any Changes Must Be On Our Part

God never changes (Heb. 13:8), and His laws never change. We are the ones who have to change. In order to prosper, we have to change from the way we have always handled our finances to the way our Father tells us to handle them. The time to do this changing is here and now, on this earth. In Heaven, we will enter into a perfect environment with no need of change.

All of God's children will enjoy His prosperity and abundance in Heaven. Prosperity obviously is not automatic. If it were, we would never see Christians with financial problems. If we want to prosper on earth, our minds must be renewed.

Our Father, like any worldly father, wants very much for His children to prosper and to be successful and healthy. In fact, His Word says that He wants this above all things.

What exactly must be done so that our souls will prosper? This question is clearly answered in verses 2 through 4 of 3 John. Instead of stopping with verse 2 as many people do, let us look at all three verses together.

> **Beloved, I wish above all things that thou mayest prosper and be in health,** *even as thy soul prospereth.* **For I rejoiced greatly, when the brethren came and testified of the truth that is in thee, even as thou walkest in the truth. I have no greater joy than to hear that my children walk in truth.**

Did you notice the five-word qualifier at the end of the second verse — **even as thy soul prospereth**? Many people who quote this verse stop with the word *health*. We must not leave out the final five words. They are the *cause* of the prosperity and health our Father wants so much for us.

The key word in those verses is *truth*. Where do we find truth? The truth is both the Living Word of God — Jesus (John 1:1) — and the revelation of God's written Word . . . **thy word is truth** (John 17:17). The Bible is the only place to find truth.

Verse 3 tells us that our Father wants His truth inside of us (in our hearts) and that He wants us to walk in truth (live our daily lives based on the teachings of His Word).

Verse 4 shows that nothing gives Him greater joy than to see His children walking in truth. We will prosper under God's laws of prosperity to the exact degree that we fill our hearts with these laws and obey them in our daily lives. This is not as easy as it might sound. Most of us have to change considerably from the way we handled our finances in the past.

The first thing to change is "thinking poor," thinking in terms of what you do not have, allowing your mind to run in the "rut" of lack. Our Father never thinks about shortages of any kind — because He has none. He does not want us to allow any such thinking into our minds, either.

If our minds are continually filled with thoughts of doubt and unbelief, how can we possibly achieve or enjoy prosperity? God wants us to restore our souls to make them brand new, changed from being permeated with the negative thinking of the world.

> **The Lord is my shepherd; I shall not want. He maketh me to lie down in green pastures: he leadeth me beside the still waters.** *He restoreth my soul* **....**
>
> **Psalm 23:1-3**

To "not be in want" means that I will not lack anything necessary for God's will to be accomplished in my life. In Jesus and in the Word of God is everything necessary for an abundant life. When the Lord is our shepherd, completely in charge of every aspect of our lives, we will not want for anything.

He will guide us to the still waters away from the angry waves of the failing systems of the world. He will bring our souls into line with His laws of prosperity and success. We will no longer frantically worry about the erosion of the world's prosperity. We must get rid of our old ways and start out anew.

> **Strip yourself of your former nature — put off and discard your old unrenewed self — which characterized your previous manner of life and becomes corrupt through lusts and desires that spring from delusion; And be constantly renewed in the spirit of your mind — having a fresh mental and spiritual attitude.**
>
> **Ephesians 4:22-23 Amp**

Too many Christians are trying to solve serious problems with limited, carnal, unrenewed minds. The information in our "computers" on which we act in normal, everyday situations *may* be all we need then; however, when a serious problem comes along, unrenewed minds are insufficient.

7
Trust God, Not Man or Self

Trust in the Lord with all thine heart; and lean not unto thine own understanding. In all thy ways acknowledge him, and he shall direct thy paths.

Proverbs 3:5-6

The second area of your mind that needs renewing is *trust*. Instead of trusting the world's wisdom and your own understanding of life and of the world systems, *you must learn to completely trust God.*

Our Father does not want us trying to figure everything out with our limited, unrenewed minds. His Word tells us that we should not rely upon our own understanding. Instead, He wants us to know what His Word says to do and then do what His Word tells us to do, trusting completely in Him.

"Trusting in the Lord with all our hearts" is the opposite of doubting God and His Word. Such trust is fundamental to our relationship with God and based on the premise that He is trustworthy. As God's children, we can be assured that our heavenly Father loves us and will faithfully care for us and guide us rightly and keep His promises.

In all our plans, decisions, and activities, we should acknowledge God as Lord and His will as our supreme desire.

57

Every day we must live in a close, trusting relationship with God, always looking to Him for direction by prayer and petition with thanksgiving.

When we do this, God promises to make our paths straight. He will lead us to His goal for our lives, remove all obstacles, and enable us to make the right choices. Christians who have not renewed their minds in God's Word do not have the spiritual insight to see their way out of seemingly unsolvable problems.

In order to solve the really difficult problems of life, we have to put on our spiritual eyeglasses. We have to see these problems as God sees them. There are no problems, financial or otherwise, that are impossible for God.

> **... With men this is impossible; but with God all things are possible** (Matt. 19:26). **I can do all things through Christ which strengtheneth me** (Phil. 4:13).

Our Father does not want us surrendering to the problems that overwhelm so many people. Jesus Christ paid the price at Calvary to give us victory over all problems.

> **... In the world ye shall have tribulation: but be of good cheer; I have overcome the world** (John 16:33). **Many are the afflictions of the righteous: but the Lord delivereth him out of them all** (Ps. 34:19).

God promised blessings and prosperity *for those who obey* His law. Our Father gave us His Word full of instructions that tell us exactly what we need to do in order to overcome the problems of this world.

He gave us His Holy Spirit to live inside of us and to guide us in the understanding of the truth that is contained in His word: **Howbeit when he, the Spirit of truth, is come, he will guide you into all truth** ... (John 16:13).

Christians who have paid the price of diligently renewing their minds will focus on the solution.

Non-Christians and Christians who have not paid the price of renewing their minds focus on the problem: **The thoughts of the diligent tend only to plenteousness; but of every one that is hasty only to want** (Prov. 21:5).

Renewal Is a Law of God

We renew our bodies each day with breakfast, lunch, and dinner. We renew ourselves each night through sleep.

God wants us to do the same things in our spiritual lives. All of us are growing older physically, and God's Word clearly tells us that we should offset this process by renewing ourselves spiritually each and every day of our lives. (2 Cor. 4:16.)

Although our bodies age and decay, we experience ongoing renewal through the constant impartation of Christ's life and power, His influence enables our minds, emotions, and will to be conformed to His likeness and eternal purpose.

In the physical world, when we eat our meals, this food is transformed into physical strength and energy. The same principles apply in the spiritual realm. We need to feed our spirits each and every day with spiritual food from God's Word. If we do this, that spiritual food is transformed into a spiritual strength and energy which is called *faith*.

We should feast on God's Word. We should stuff ourselves with it. Jesus told us we should feed ourselves with every word from our Father so that we can live our lives as He wants us to live them.

> **But he answered and said, It is written, Man shall not live by bread alone, but by every word that proceedeth out of the mouth of God.**
>
> **Matthew 4:4**

If we do this spiritual feeding on a regular and continuing basis, regardless of what we might be going through on the outside, we will always be full of joy on the inside.

Thy words were found, and I did eat them; and thy word was unto me the joy and rejoicing of mine heart: for I am called by thy name, O Lord God of hosts.

Jeremiah 15:16

Jeremiah loved the Word of the Lord, just as we must. It should be a joy and delight to our hearts. One sure sign that we are children of God is an intense love for God's inspired Word. He does not want our imaginations running rampant about the financial problems of the world and how bad they might become.

He wants our minds renewed to the point where they can cast down negative thoughts and focus totally on the promises in His Word.

Casting down imaginations, and every high thing that exalteth itself against the knowledge of God, and bringing into captivity every thought to the obedience of Christ.

2 Corinthians 10:5

Use these following four steps to bring your thought life under Christ's Lordship:

1. *Be aware that God knows every thought* and that nothing is hidden from Him: **The Lord knoweth the thoughts of man, that they are vanity** (Ps. 94:11). We will have to give account to God for our thoughts as we will our words and deeds.

2. *Be aware that the mind is a battleground.* Some thoughts originate with us, while others come directly from the enemy. To "take captive every thought" requires warfare against both our sinful nature and satanic forces.

For we wrestle not against flesh and blood, but against principalities, against powers, against the rulers of the darkness of this world, against spiritual

wickedness in high places. Wherefore take unto you the whole armour of God, that ye may be able to withstand in the evil day, and having done all, to stand.

Ephesians 6:12,13

We must steadfastly resist and reject evil and unwholesome thoughts in the name of the Lord Jesus Christ. Remember that, as believers, we overcome our adversary by the blood of the Lamb, by the word of our testimony, and by persistently saying no to the devil, temptations, and sin. (Rev. 12:11.)

3. *Be resolute in focusing your mind on Christ* and heavenly things rather than on earthly things, for the mind controlled by the spirit is life and peace.

Fill your mind with God's Word and with those things that are noble, excellent, and praiseworthy. Always be careful what your eyes see and your ears hear. Refuse to let your eyes be an instrument for lust, or to set any worthless or evil thing before your eyes, whether in books, magazines, pictures, television programs, or in real life.

4. Be steadfast in fixing your mind on positive things.

Finally, brethren, whatsoever things are true, whatsoever things are honest, whatsoever things are just, whatsoever things are pure, whatsoever things are lovely, whatsoever things are of good report; if there be any virtue, and if there be any praise, think on these things.

Philippians 4:8

If you fix your mind on those things that Paul mentions to the Philippians, you will have peace and freedom. The "God of peace" will be with you. (Phil. 4:9.) Our Father has more than enough to meet every one of our needs. God is not dependent in any way upon the condition of man's economic system!

If we do not continually renew our minds, they are wide open to doubts, fears, and anxieties about situations that surround us. Our souls cannot prosper unless our minds are under control, and our minds will not be under control until we cast out negative imaginations and bring every thought completely in line with the Word of God.

If our minds are properly renewed, we will decide what we are going to think about. We will refuse to let any external situation control our thought process. Too many Christians focus so much on the problems of the world that they ultimately become part of those problems through identifying with them. Instead, we need to redirect our attention to God's solutions.

We can live peaceful, joyous, prosperous, healthy lives in this world. Jesus Christ has paid the price for our peace, our joy, our prosperity, and our health. However, once again, this peace, joy, prosperity, and health are not automatic. We will experience them only to the degree that we renew our minds on a daily, continuing basis.

In order for us to prosper as our Father wants us to prosper, our souls must prosper.

In order for our souls to prosper, God's Word must dominate our lives. God's instructions to us must be the absolute center of our lives. Everything we think, say, and do must revolve around His instruction to us.

May the God of hope fill you with all joy and peace as you trust in him, so that you may overflow with hope by the power of the Holy Spirit.

Romans 15:13 NIV

8

Live in the World, but Don't Act Like It

Don't copy the behavior and customs of this world, but be a new and different person with a fresh newness in all you do and think. Then you will learn from your own experience how his ways will really satisfy you.

Romans 12:2 TLB

Now that we have seen our Father wants us to renew our minds, we need to see exactly how He tells us to do this: We renew our minds through constant study and meditation in God's Word. *We must live in this world, but we do not have to act like this world.* Christians are the true "aliens" on earth.

If I could speak personally to each reader of this book, I would ask you, "Do you want God to approve of what you do?"

You undoubtedly would say, "Yes, of course I do."

Here is how we win our Father's approval:

Study to shew thyself approved unto God, a workman that needeth not to be ashamed, rightly dividing the word of truth.

2 Timothy 2:15

We win God's approval by studying His Word!

We win His approval by working hard enough at this study that we will not be ashamed. Do you believe God has approved of your Bible study during the week? During the past month? During the past year? Are you ashamed at the small amount of time you spend studying the instructions our Father has given to us?

There is no easy way. Bible study in hard work. None of us should expect our Father to prosper us unless we are willing to pay the price of working hard at studying His Word. In fact, the Greek word *spoundazo*, translated *study* in 2 Timothy 2:15, means "exertion, or diligence." In Hebrews 4:11 this same Greek word is translated *labour*.

There is no question our Father expects us to work hard studying His Word. Everything any of us will ever need to know is contained in God's Word. If we have problems in one particular area of our lives, we need to do a thorough job of "rightly dividing" God's Word in order to find every possible verse of scripture that covers that particular area.

Studying the Bible is not a "high-flying" supernatural experience. There are a few times like this, but Bible study is often laborious and tedious. This is especially true for someone who is not accustomed to studying.

It is difficult to get started and usually takes quite a while to learn how to enjoy Bible study. Unfortunately, most Christians quit before they get to that point. The Bible will make us think as we have never thought before, but only if we are willing to dig and dig and dig without expecting it to unfold its secrets immediately.

What is the difference between *studying* the Bible and just reading it? To study the Bible, you must be serious about how to get acquainted with its contents. You must devour every fact in it that could possibly show you the true meaning.

It is particularly important at this time in history to learn everything we possibly can about how to avoid or solve the financial problems that I believe soon will come upon this world.

Millions of Christians are living far beneath their rights and privileges as children of God, because they fail to pay the price of constantly studying God's Word to find out what their rights and privileges are and how to attain them.

Specifically and exactly, how do we go about studying the Bible?

This is a subject that would make a book by itself. I do not believe there is only one "right" method of studying God's Word. The methods may vary considerably, but I have found that principles of effective Bible study are similar regardless of the method used.

Bible concordances, topical Bibles, Bible dictionaries, Greek and Hebrew lexicons are available, as well as other Bible study tools. All of these help us find every possible verse of scripture on any given subject and then understand exactly what these verses mean.

In this book, I have dug out dozens of verses on the subject of financial prosperity and success. I have explained what these verses of scripture mean, so this part has already been done for you on this subject.

A Threefold Principle: Study, Meditate, Do

Next, we need to know what it means to meditate on these verses of scripture. Let us start by looking at two verses that tie the words *meditate* and *prosper* together. The first one says:

> **This book of the law shall not depart out of thy mouth; but thou shalt meditate therein day and night, that thou mayest observe to do according to all that is written therein: for then thou shalt make thy way**

***prosperous* and then thou shalt have good *success*.**

Joshua 1:8

Joshua was to be faithful to God's Word by talking about it, meditating on it, and obeying it fully. Meditate means "to read quietly or to talk to yourself as you think." It involves reflecting on God's Word and ways and applying them to every area of your life.

Those who know and obey God's Word and law will be prosperous and successful in that they possess the wisdom to live righteously and to achieve God's goal for their lives. Make God's Word your authoritative guide for all beliefs and action.

Joshua 1:8 is one of the most important verses of scripture in the entire Bible for anyone interested in prosperity and success. In fact, it is the only verse which contains both the words *prosperous* and *success*.

I have worked with many Christians in the area of prosperity and success, and this verse has been one of the most significant in showing them the three things our Father has told us to do if we intend to be prosperous and successful:

1. *Be strong in the Word and in faith.* We must speak His Word constantly. His scriptures should constantly come out of our mouths. We must constantly study His Word and meditate day and night on what it says in order for it to automatically come out of our mouths.

2. *Be courageous in following God's will.* Those seeking to live under God's blessing meditate on God's law (His Word) in order to shape their thinking and actions. They read the words of Scripture, ponder them, compare them with other scriptures, then act on what they have learned.

3. *Be diligent in obeying His instructions.* We must constantly live our lives exactly as His Word tells us. We should

know His Word well enough to conduct our lives according to all that is written therein.

The second place we find scripture that ties meditation with prosperity together is in the first psalm:

Blessed is the man that walketh not in the counsel of the ungodly, nor standeth in the way of sinners, nor sitteth in the seat of the scornful. But his delight is in the law of the Lord; and in his law doth he meditate day and night. And he shall be like a tree planted by the rivers of water, that bringeth forth his fruit in his season; his leaf also shall not wither; and whatsoever he doeth shall prosper.

Psalm 1:1-3

True believers can be distinguished by the things they do *not* do, the places they do *not* go and the company they do *not* keep. No one can experience God's blessings without turning from those things that are harmful or destructive. Those who are blessed by God not only turn from evil, but build their lives around the words of the Lord. They seek to obey God's will out of hearts that genuinely take pleasure in His ways and commands.

David told us that God will bless us if we follow His laws of prosperity and success instead of following the world's methods. God does not want us living the way the sinful world lives. He does not want us looking at things the way worldly people do. We must love His Word so much that we actually have such great delight in it that we cannot get enough.

We will be so hungry and thirsty spiritually that we will meditate day and night in His Word to find out everything we possibly can about our Father's laws for living our lives.

What will happen to us if we do this? The psalmist wrote that we will be like trees planted next to a river. (Ps. 1:3.) No matter how bad a drought might be, the leaves of such a tree will never wither and dry up, because its roots will be able to draw water from the river. No matter how long a drought occurs, the trees next to a river will continue to bear fruit.

Many economists believe that a "financial drought" is coming over our land. Inflation, recession, unemployment and all the rest are already causing our economy to start to wither.

How To Live Through a Drought

In the midst of such a drought, Christians can still thrive. We can still bear fruit. We can still prosper in everything we do, if we have meditated day and night in God's Word so that our roots reach deep into our Father's laws of prosperity and success.

Unfortunately, many Christians will wither during this financial drought. Many Christians will be destroyed because of lack of knowledge of God's laws. God Himself said: **My people are destroyed for lack of knowledge . . .** (Hosea 4:6).

Lack of personal knowledge of God will keep you from prospering. Even today within the church some are being destroyed by the sinful ways of the world, because they do not know God and His inspired Word.

If Christians want to be delivered from this financial drought, they can be — in exact proportion to their knowledge of God's laws of prosperity: **. . . but through knowledge shall the just be delivered** (Prov. 11:9).

Now that we have seen how Joshua 1:8 and Psalm 1:1-3 tie prosperity and *meditation* together, let us look at this word meditation in more detail. Exactly what does meditation mean, and exactly how do we go about meditating in God's Word?

Once again, I do not believe there is any specific way of doing this that is the only right way. However, I would like to share with you a system of meditation that has worked wonderfully for me and many other Christians who have followed it.

The system starts with reading and studying the Bible in order to find every possible verse of scripture on one topic, in this case the subject of financial prosperity and success. Once all of these verses of scripture are found, begin the process of meditation by typing or writing each verse on a 3-by-5 file card that will fit easily into a man's shirt pocket or a woman's purse.

Arrange your cards in the order of their importance, i.e., the ones that mean the most to you on top, the next most important verses in the middle of the stack, and so forth. Next, *and this is important*, take just one of these cards at a time.

Do not give yourself "spiritual indigestion" by trying to digest too much of God's Word at one time. Take only one verse of scripture with you and meditate on that one verse throughout that day or week. Do not rush. God is never in a hurry. He wants us to be calm and quiet in our meditation in His Word.

I believe meditation means to fix our attention on a particular verse of scripture and turn this verse over and over in our minds, looking at it from every angle.

I believe meditation means to "personalize" a verse of scripture — to think deeply about how each particular verse applies to our own lives. When we meditate on a verse of scripture, our thought processes should be something like this:

• What does this verse of scripture mean?

• What is God telling me? Exactly how does this apply to my life?

• What change do I need to make in order to do what God is telling me to do?

• What am I going to do differently today? This week? This month? During the next year?

This is so beautiful. Unlike the "meditation" practices of Eastern mysticism, New Age groups, and false religions, which teach you to "empty your mind," Christians are to meditate by *filling our minds* with the awesome power of the Word of God. As we meditate more and more on God's Word, we are brought more and more in touch with our Creator.

Of course, this process of daily meditation is not easy at first. When we are not used to something, it takes time for it to become part of our habit patterns. Be patient with this system of meditation. Give it a fair chance to become part of your daily lifestyle.

Most readers have jobs that require them to work about eight hours a day. This means most of you cannot study God's Word through the day. However, you can meditate on it constantly. You can meditate while getting dressed in the morning, driving to work, during your lunch hour, and while driving home.

Meditate Means "To Repeat Over and Over"

Some people work at occupations that enable them to meditate while they are working. In addition, all of us have discretionary time at the end of each day and on weekends that can be used to meditate. During these times, we also should speak the verse out loud, if possible, over and over.

In fact, the Hebrew word translated *meditate* in Joshua 1:8 and Psalms 1:2 actually means "to murmur or to mutter." When God's Word tells us to meditate day and night, this means we should constantly open our mouths and speak the verse of scripture on which we are meditating.

As we constantly speak a verse of scripture, this helps us to memorize it. Also, as we constantly speak a verse of scripture, this releases the power of that verse of scripture. Be sure to meditate on just one verse at a time.

Turn it over and over in your mind. Think how it applies to your particular need. Say it out loud — over and over and over — until it becomes a part of you, until that verse has gone from your Bible to your file card to your mind and then down into your heart. Do not rush this process. If you finish only one verse a week, you will have 52 great teachings from God deep in your heart at the end of a year.

This system has worked beautifully in my life for the past 25 years. I have worked with several people who have followed this method, and the results have been exceptional in their lives, also. I meet many Christians who know I follow this system, and they smile and pull out the file card they are carrying that particular day.

To someone whose mind has not been renewed, this might sound like a lot of drudgery. However, God's Word tells us this continuous meditation eventually will be just the opposite of drudgery. What will happen if we delight in the Word and meditate day and night in it, as David wrote? Here is the answer:

> . . . **Blessed is the man that feareth the Lord, that delighteth greatly in his commandments. His seed shall be mighty upon the earth: the generation of the upright shall be blessed. Wealth and riches shall be in his house: and his righteousness endureth forever.**
>
> **Psalms 112:1-3**

God's Word should be an absolute delight to us because His Word tells us everything any of us will ever need to know in order to live good lives here on this earth.

> **For as you know Him better, he will give you, through his great power, everything you need for living a truly good life: he even shares his own glory and his own goodness with us!**
>
> **2 Peter 1:3 TLB**

God met the needs of His people Israel, and He met the needs of the early Church. His principles are just as adequate today. Absolutely nothing can offer more height, depth, strength, and help than Jesus provides. Once we fully understand what this means to us, we will not be able to get enough of God's Word.

If we gladly meditate on His Word continually, we will prosper in every area of our lives — financially, spiritually, physically, mentally, and emotionally.

9

Work and Discipline:
A Channel for Prosperity
and Success

... Work with your hands, as we charged you; so that you may bear yourselves becomingly, be correct and honorable and command the respect of the outside world, being (self-supporting) dependent on nobody and having need of nothing.

1 Thessalonians 4:11-12 Amp

God's Word repeatedly tells us that He expects us to work and discipline ourselves, if we want to lead prosperous, successful lives.

For some reason, many Christians believe they can have anything they ask for in Jesus' name without having to work hard. This is incorrect. God's Word clearly tells us that we need to do the very best we can with the abilities God has given us. *Then* we can stand solidly on our faith in Him to take care of the rest. (Eph. 6:13.)

The believer's victory has been secured by Christ himself through His death on the cross. Jesus waged a triumphant battle

73

against Satan, disarmed the evil powers and authorities, and redeemed the believer from Satan's power.

> **Wherefore thou art no more a servant, but a son; and if a son, then an heir of God through Christ.**
>
> **Galatians 4:7**

However, God's laws of prosperity and success definitely require us to work hard if we want to prosper. We cannot spend our lives on "flowery beds of ease" and receive blessings due us as sons. We must do our parts: *receive* the blessings and *do* what our hands find to do to make a way for them to reach us.

God "worked" six days and rested the seventh as a pattern for us, although work was a pleasure and a joy in the Garden. After the fall, it became hard and "by the sweat of one's brow." (Gen. 3:17-19.) Nevertheless, work is a part of God's will for His children.

God said He had "given" the Israelites the Promised Land, yet they still had to work and fight to take it. The Creator wants His children to have a part in His purposes. We cannot "earn" by works or good behavior the things that are only His to give out of love and mercy: salvation, rewards in Heaven, and the blessings of health and well-being.

On the other hand, He will not carry us as babies when it would hinder us from learning to walk, from growing up. Our part is to hear His Word and obey. Part of that obedience is to work at whatever He assigns us to do. That includes making a living or maintaining and expanding for His glory whatever riches we have, financially or spiritually.

The "work ethic," so much a part of the beliefs and lives of the founding fathers of the United States, is biblical. A topical Bible (one with references arranged by subjects or categories) will show clearly what God thinks of work and those who do not work.

Today's Society Focuses on Leisure

Today, however, the "work ethic" upon which this country was founded has eroded more and more with the passage of time. On the whole, there is much more of a "the-world-owes-me-a-living" attitude than there was even a generation ago. Many people put as little into their work as they can get away with.

This is one of the primary reasons why the American economy is in trouble. There are too many employees receiving a full day's pay for less than a full day's work. This cost is passed on to the consumer and is one of the primary causes of inflation. More and more emphasis is being placed on fun, enjoyment, and leisure — on a "me first, what-do-I-want-to-do-to-please-myself-today attitude."

Many people have been able to get by with this type of attitude since World War II, but I believe there will be much more necessity to work hard in the years immediately ahead of us than there has been in most of our lifetimes.

God's Word says if any would not work, neither should he eat. (2 Thess. 3:10.) This obvious truth has been contradicted by the top-heavy, unbalanced systems developed as welfare programs, and by government agencies, and some labor unions.

The foundational goals of these systems were predicated upon basic Christian principles. However, self-seeking leaders, consumed by greed and corruption, have made the organizations or agencies a mockery of what the founders intended.

The price is now about to be paid. In the United States, we live in a society that virtually has done away with having to work in order to eat. Many people at the bottom of the economic ladder in the United States have color television sets, more than

75

adequate living quarters, and more than the basic necessities of life. That would be fine, if they had earned what they have.

However, many of these people do not work and would not if they were given an opportunity to work. If we want to succeed, we need to eliminate the short cuts that are like "band aids" on the "cancer" of poverty. If we want to succeed, we must work hard and diligently.

God's Word reveals in many places that His children should work hard and show the world around them the virtues of hard work:

> **He becometh poor that dealeth with a slack hand: but the hand of the diligent maketh rich** (Prov. 10:4). **Seest thou a man diligent in his business? He shall stand before kings; he shall not stand before mean men** (Prov. 22:29).

A Day of Reckoning Is Coming

Today, many people have little or no initiative. The sluggard or lazy person is one who puts off beginning what he or she should do, does not finish what has been started, and follows the least difficult course of action. Slothfulness, or laziness, is as prevalent in the spiritual realm as in the physical.

God exhorts us to make our calling and election sure with all eagerness. The day of reckoning is drawing near. Proverbs 6:9-11 tells us that one day lazy people will wake up to find poverty has overtaken them like an armed robber and is taking everything they have — homes, cars, and anything else they own.

We cannot continue to violate God's laws. No matter how "square" they might seem to the society in which we live, these laws are from God. We may get away with breaking His laws for a while, but sooner or later, we are going to pay the price.

Employers cannot continue to pay people more than they are worth. Sooner or later the bubble has to burst.

Already, this philosophy has resulted in widespread unemployment in several industries where wages of both skilled and unskilled workers have been driven to a much higher level than is justified. If we constantly try to get more than our work is worth, we violate God's laws of prosperity and success.

In fact, God clearly instructs us to go in the opposite direction. Instead of robbing our employer by doing less than we are capable of doing, God's Word tells us to work as hard as we possibly can: **Whatsoever thy hand findeth to do, do it with all thy might . . .** (Eccl. 9:10).

Instead of doing less than we are required to do, our Lord wants us to do *more* than we have to do. If we need to go one mile, Jesus told us we should go two miles. (Matt. 5:41.) In other words, we are to do twice as much as we are required to do. This is just the opposite of the prevailing attitude today.

Many people are looking for ideal working conditions, longer vacations, more leisure, and more benefits. God's Word tells us to get out and do our jobs whether or not it is cold, wet, or otherwise uncomfortable. If we do not do this, we will not receive any lasting gain.

> **The sluggard will not plow by reason of the cold; therefore shall he beg in harvest, and have nothing.**
>
> **Proverbs 20:4**

Whatever type of work any of us might do, God's Word tells us we should put everything we have into it, because we really are working for Jesus Christ, not worldly employers: **And whatsoever ye do, do it heartily, as to the Lord, and not unto men** (Col. 3:23).

Paul exhorted Christians to regard all labor as a service rendered to the Lord. We must work as though Christ were our employer, knowing that all work performed *for the Lord* will be rewarded. God's Word tells us to do our work "heartily." This means to work from our hearts, our spirits, our innermost beings. That is where the Holy Spirit lives.

If we allow Him to take charge of our work, we will do a great job no matter in what line of work we find ourselves. The Holy Spirit is the world's best salesman, mechanic, factory worker, engineer, nurse and doctor or dentist, and the world's best at any other occupation. There is no limit to what He can do through us. Our job is to do the very best we can with our human abilities and trust in Him for the rest.

If a Christian does not do his best at this work, he soon starts to get an empty feeling. This comes from the Holy Spirit inside "nudging" him to get to work. On the other hand, when we put in a good solid day's work, we get a sense of inner satisfaction. This is because way down deep, we know that we are doing what our Father wants us to do.

God wants us to do our best. However, the fact remains that the great things of life really are done *through* us, not *by* us: **Except the Lord build the house, they labour in vain that buildit . . .** (Ps. 127:1).

As we labor to build God's house on earth, we must make sure we build it according to His pattern and by His Spirit, not according to mere human ideas, plans, and effort. God will do great things through us if we will first of all do our very best and then trust completely in Him to take it from there.

Many Christians miss out by going to one extreme or the other. Either we do not do our best, or we think we have to do everything by ourselves and do not "let go and let God." Hard work starts with discipline. If we want to be free from financial problems or any other problems, we must have the discipline to continually study God's Word.

Then said Jesus to those Jews which believed on him, If ye continue in my Word, then are ye my disciples

indeed; And ye shall know the truth, and the truth shall make you free.

John 8:31,32

In the context of human knowledge, many things are true. Yet there is only one truth that will set people free from sin, destruction, and Satan's dominion — the truth of Jesus Christ found in God's Word.

I would ask each reader, "Do you want to be a disciple of Jesus Christ? Do you want to be free?"

We have just seen that this freedom is obtained by continuing in God's Word day after day, week after week, and month after month. In my opinion, the primary thing that stops Christians from realizing the freedom that is theirs in Christ is lack of consistency.

Many Christians begin to study God's Word, but there are not as many Christians who continually study and meditate in God's Word. The words *disciple* and *discipline* come from the same root. This is not a coincidence. If we really want to be disciples of Jesus Christ, we must have the discipline to get into God's Word and stay there.

True Disciples Love His Word

We will only do what God's Word tells us if we get into His "perfect law of liberty" — the law that sets us free — and continually study and meditate in these laws. If we do this we will be blessed by our Father.

But whoso looketh into the perfect law of liberty, and continueth therein, he being not a forgetful hearer, but a doer of the Word, this man shall be blessed in his deed.

James 1:25

This law is the will of God internalized in our hearts by the indwelling Holy Spirit. Through faith in Christ we receive

79

not only mercy and forgiveness, but also the power and freedom to obey God's law. It is called the "law that gives freedom," because the believer desires freely to do God's will. It must never be viewed as a freedom to violate Christ's commands, but rather as the freedom and power to obey them.

If it takes four years to graduate from high school and another four years to graduate from college, why should we expect to learn God's great spiritual laws without spending a great deal of time and effort studying and meditating? If we want God to prosper us, we must give ourselves wholly to continual study and meditating in His Word.

Meditate upon these things; give thyself wholly to them; that thy profiting may appear to all.

1 Timothy 4:15

Many Christians decide they are going to pay the price of continuous spiritual study and meditation, but they do not keep their resolve. The first four or five weeks are the hardest. If you can stick to a definite pattern of study and meditation for at least that long, you will start to develop habit patterns that will last.

Some Christians believe disciplined study and meditation is contrary to a life led by the Holy Spirit.

They say, "I'm not going to grind it out every day. I'm going to wait on the Holy Spirit each day and do what He leads me to do."

The Holy Spirit never leads us contrary to the Word, and God's Word tells us again and again about the absolute importance of disciplining ourselves to study and meditate constantly in His Word. Satan wants us to have sloppy day-to-day habits with no set pattern. Our Father wants us to realize how precious our time is: **Teach us to number our days and recognize how few they are; help us to spend them as we should** (Ps. 90:12 TLB).

Our Father does not want us to waste our time on earth. He wants us to make good use of it. It helps to look on the days of your life as a "bank account" opened for you when you are born. Each year, you "spend" a dollar, and you only have 40 or 60 or 80-some, perhaps. That concept helps us think about how each "dollar" is spent and how few there really are.

> **Look carefully then how you walk! Live purposefully and worthily and accurately, not as the unwise and witless, but as wise — sensible intelligent people; Making the very most of the time — buying up each opportunity — because the days are evil.**
>
> **Ephesians 5:15,16 Amp**

Next, let us see what God's Word says about the results diligent study and meditation will produce in our hearts, in our mouths, and in our actions.

10

Head Knowledge Will Not Activate God's Laws

Wisdom and knowledge is granted unto thee; and I will give thee riches, and wealth, and honour....

2 Chronicles 1:12

When we hear God's Word spoken, it sows a seed in our hearts. Unfortunately, many people hear God's inspired Word in church, but have forgotten most of what they heard before they reach their parked automobiles. When this happens, the seed of God's Word never has the opportunity to take root and grow. God's Word will only grow in our hearts to the degree that we constantly meditate on it.

Head knowledge is not sufficient to achieve any of God's laws.

God's laws come from a spiritual realm that is completely different from the natural world in which we live. We cannot understand God's laws with our minds or human understanding. The key to activating His laws is to get them down in our hearts: **For as he thinketh in his heart, so is he ...** (Prov. 23:7).

This is why God wants us to meditate day and night in His Word. This will change every aspect of our lives, because the significant events in our lives are based upon what we believe deep down in our hearts. (Prov. 4:23). The heart is the well-spring of desire and decision.

Following God and knowing His ways involve a resolute decision to remain committed to Him, seeking first His kingdom and His righteousness.

If we find that our hunger and thirst for God and His kingdom are declining, we should reevaluate our priorities, honestly acknowledge our lukewarmness, and earnestly pray for a renewed desire for God to have His favor.

Failure to guard our hearts results in a departure from the path of safety and entrapment in a destructive snare; to watch over our hearts above all else results in a firm walk on a level path through His favor and grace. Our Father wants our hearts and minds filled with His Word: **Therefore shall ye lay up these my words in your heart and in your soul . . .** (Deut. 11:18).

Constant meditation on God's Word causes the scripture to drop from our minds down into our hearts. As this process takes place, the problems that used to baffle us will not trip us up any more: **The law of his God is in his heart; none of his steps shall slide** (Ps. 37:31).

As I have mentioned, in difficult economic times, many people try to stockpile money and hoard up food and other necessities of life. This urge to store up is actually a counterfeit of the spiritual "storing up" that our Father wants us to do in such times. He wants us to fill our hearts to overflowing with His Word, so that we will react instinctively whenever we are faced with a crisis. Our Father wants His Word to be so solidly established in our hearts that we will not be afraid of any problem that comes upon us.

Surely he shall not be moved for ever: the righteous shall be in everlasting remembrance. He shall not be afraid of evil tidings: his heart is fixed, trusting in the Lord. His heart is established, he shall not be afraid . . . .

Psalm 112:6-8

We should not be moved by fear and anxiety in times of trouble, because our trust is in the Lord, not in ourselves or in external circumstances. We should never be afraid of evil tidings. Instead of focusing on bad news about inflation, unemployment, or interest rates, our hearts should be "fixed" on God's Word, trusting completely in His promises.

No matter how bad the situation might look, a truly established heart will never waver. Our Father wants our minds and hearts to be so full of His Word that it will overcome any problem that comes into our lives: **So mightily grew the Word of God and prevailed** (Acts 19:20).

The Greek word translated *prevail* means "to be strong and powerful." Our Father wants His Word to be so strong and powerful inside of us that it will prevail over every problem. There is nothing to fear. There is no need to worry. No matter how bad a situation might seem to be, God will always come through to the exact degree that we believe in Him in our hearts.

God will do His part, if we do our part. Our part is to get enough of His Word in our hearts to be able to trust totally and completely in Him.

The Lord is good, a strong hold in the day of trouble; and he knoweth them that trust in him.

Nahum 1:7

Our hearts are where the "software" data from the Word of God is stored for use in our brain-computers. When a problem comes into our lives, the "data-retrieval" function of our minds should immediately turn to the storage area in our hearts and search out the appropriate laws of God to affect the problem. Then, we should respond based upon our faith in what God's Word says and not based upon the problem with which we are confronted.

Look at Solutions, Not Problems

No matter how difficult the problem might seem to be, we should trust the Lord. God does not want us to be *careful*. This Old English word used in the *King James Bible* does not mean the same as the word "careful" does today. *Careful* to English-speaking folks of King James' day meant "to be full of care, to be worried, or anxious" (care-full).

When difficult problems come into our lives, instead of being full of worries and cares, our Father wants us to go to Him with a prayer of faith based solidly upon the promises in His Word. If we really trust Him, our prayers will be thanks more than requests, because we know He will do what His Word says He will do.

If we follow these instructions, when trouble comes into our lives God's Word says that we will receive a peace beyond our human understanding.

> **Be careful for nothing; but in every thing by prayer and supplication with thanksgiving let your request be made known unto God. And the peace of God, which passeth all understanding, shall keep your hearts and minds through Christ Jesus.**
>
> **Philippians 4:6,7**

The one essential cure for worry is prayer for the following reason: Through prayer we renew our trust in the Lord's faithfulness by casting all our anxieties and problems on Him who cares for us.

God's peace comes to guard our hearts and minds as a result of communion with Jesus. If we really trust God in our hearts, we will show this trust by the words that come out of our mouths. We have seen a good example of this regarding our prayers in times of adversity. If our hearts are filled to overflowing with God's Word, this abundance of scripture will come out of our mouths. Jesus told us this when he said:

> **... For out of the abundance of the heart the mouth speaketh. A good man out of the good treasure of the heart bringeth forth good things: and an evil man out of the evil treasure bringeth forth evil things.**
>
> **Matthew 12:34,35**

In times of extreme pressure, we will show what fills our hearts by the words that come out of our mouths. God's Word tells us what happens when we allow the wrong words to come out of our mouths: **If any man among you seem to be religious, and bridleth not his tongue, but deceiveth his own heart, this man's religion is vain** (James 1:26).

The Greek word translated *vain* means "to be void of results." Thus, if we do not "bridle" our tongues (keep them under control), our words can cause our blessings to be ineffective or void. If we constantly speak words contrary to God's laws, this implies doubt and lack of faith.

Our heavenly Father will not prosper us without faith. He has established His Kingdom to operate on faith. Without faith, no one receives anything from God, beginning with salvation. (Heb. 11:6.)

Many Christians put themselves into financial prison and throw away the key by the words of fear and doubt that come out of their mouths when faced with a crisis. They do not realize that God's Word says: **Thou art snared with the words of thy mouth, thou art taken with the words of thy mouth** (Prov. 6:2).

A "snare" is a trap, and many of us are trapped by our words without even realizing it. Our words can put us into financial prison or they can set us free: **Whoso keepeth his mouth and his tongue keepeth his soul from troubles** (Prov. 21:23). However, in moments of stress, we cannot control our tongues with sheer will power: **But the tongue can no man tame . . .** (James 3:8).

The Heart Controls Behavior

When the going is tough, we cannot control what we say by our minds. Our words are totally controlled by what we believe in our hearts. This is why it is so important for our hearts to be filled with God's Word. Do you remember our discussion of Joshua 1:8 — the only verse of scripture in the entire Bible that mentions both *success* and *prosperous*?

This verse begins with the words: **This book of the law shall not depart out of thy mouth.** This means that, if we expect to prosper, we should speak God's Word all day long every day of our lives. It should not ever depart from our mouths. I ask each reader to be honest and answer the following two questions:

• Do I really speak the Word of God all day long from the time I get up in the morning until the time that I go to bed at night?

• Do I do this day after day, week after week, and month after month?

God's Word is greater than any problem we will ever face. In the spiritual realm, God's Word, when spoken and backed by strong, patient, unwavering faith, has the same power as if God spoke aloud.

So shall my Word be that goeth forth out of my mouth: it shall not return unto me void, but is shall accomplish that which I please, and it shall prosper in the thing whereto I sent it.

Isaiah 55:11

The power and/or effect of God's Word are never canceled or rendered void. His Word will bring either spiritual life to those who receive it or condemnation to those who reject it. We can clearly see that God's Word ties together the words we speak with our mouths and the prosperity we receive in our lives. God will prosper us if we deeply believe His promises in our hearts and constantly open our mouths and speak these promises.

We should never talk about tight money, hard times, or other financial problems. If we allow these words to come out of our mouths, we are actually denying the promises of God. How can we expect our Father to bless us if we constantly open our mouths and deny the promises He has given to us?

I urge each reader of this book to apply this concept to the procedure we covered previously. Take a verse of scripture on a 3-by-5 file card with you each day. Meditate on this verse of scripture throughout the day and night. Turn it over and over in your mind. Think exactly how this applies to your life.

Above all else, open your mouth and boldly speak this verse of scripture over and over and over. When the going is tough, we need to speak God's Word more and more and more. When I was on the very edge of bankruptcy and a nervous breakdown, I used to say and read my favorite verse of scripture (Phil. 4:13) over and over.

I can remember dark and dreary days when I would sit down at my desk and repeat, **I can do all things through Christ which strengtheneth me**, 100 times. Every time I said this verse, I wrote down the number of times I had spoken it on a pad — 1,2,3,4, etc. This was not easy. Try it sometime and see for yourself.

God's Word tells us how our faith grows: **So then faith cometh by hearing, and hearing by the word of God**

(Rom. 10:17). We are told also that some people hear God's Word and do not profit.

For unto us was the gospel preached, as well as unto them: but the word preached did not profit them, not being mixed with faith in them that heard it.

Hebrews 4:2

Hearing God's Word will only profit us to the degree that we undergird it with faith. How do we "mix the Word with faith"? The answer is that we must *speak* what we believe and *act* on what we believe. I am absolutely convinced faith grows more rapidly when our ears hear our own mouths constantly speaking God's Word.

When we face difficult problems our words must express our faith. We must not waver. We must hold fast to the confession of God's Word, because we know that our Father will do exactly what His Word says He will do: **Let us hold fast the profession of our faith without wavering; (for He is faithful that promised)** (Heb. 10:23).

We are all human. We are not perfect. We might slip and allow something negative to come out of our mouths. If this happens, we should go immediately to our Father and confess the error of our ways and ask Him to forgive us. He will do this.

If we confess our sins, He is faithful and just to forgive us our sins, and to cleanse us from all unrighteousness.

1 John 1:9

We must admit our sins and seek forgiveness and purifying from God. The two results are 1) forgiveness and reconciliation with God, and 2) the purifying from (removal of) guilt and the destruction of the power of sin in order to live lives of holiness.

If we ask our Father to forgive us, He will. He will completely cleanse us from these words. He will render them

90

null and void. It will be as if they were never spoken. He will forget that we said them.

For I will be merciful to their unrighteousness, and their sins and their iniquities will I remember no more.

Hebrews 8:12

11

Act on What You Know

Therefore whosoever heareth these sayings of mine, and doeth them, I will liken him unto a wise man, which built his house upon a rock: And the rains descended, and the flood came, and the winds blew, and beat upon that house; and it fell not: for it was founded upon a rock.

Matthew 7:24,25

The time has now arrived to look at the final instruction of Joshua 1:8, the "prosperity and success scripture." That verse tells us to meditate day and night in God's Word, to speak God's Word constantly, and to do according to all that is written therein.

Jesus Christ placed great emphasis on the importance of doing what God's Word tells us to do. He continued by explaining what happens to those who hear His words and do *not* do them.

And every one that heareth these sayings of mine, and doeth them not, shall be likened unto a foolish man, which built his house upon the sand: And the rain descended, and the floods came, and the winds blew, and beat upon that house; and it fell: and great was the fall of it.

Matthew 7:26,27

93

Many economists predict that great economic storms will be coming upon us before too long. Will you fall under the pressure of these storms? Jesus says we will not fall, if we do what His Word tells us to do, because then our foundation is built on "solid rock." However, it is a sad fact that many Christians hear God's Word, but fail to do what it says.

When this happens, Jesus said we are building on a shaky foundation of sand, and we will fall. Our financial future in a shaky economy will finally come down to one great truth: Are we actually doing what God's Word tells us to do?

Obedience is the key to receiving God's blessing: . . . **Blessed are they that hear the Word of God, and keep it** (Luke 11:28). Many Christians fail to receive their Father's blessing simply because they do not step out in faith in obedience to what His Word says to do. This is what "separates the men from the boys" spiritually. Strong faith demands action.

If we really believe, then we will do exactly what our Father's Word tells us to do: **But be ye doers of the Word, and not hearers only, deceiving your own selves** (James 1:22). If we just listen to God's Word and do not do what it says to do, we deceive ourselves!

Why does God tell us to fill our hearts and our mouths with His Word? He tells us this for one reason: **But the Word is very nigh unto thee, in thy mouth, and in thy heart, that thou mayest do it** (Deut. 30:14). When we surrender our lives to Jesus Christ, we are given a recreated spirit, a brand new spiritual heart. This new heart will cause us to want to do what God's Word tells us to do.

A new heart also will I give you, and a new spirit will I put within you: and I will take away the stony heart out of your flesh, and I will give you a heart of flesh. And I will put my spirit within you, and cause you to

walk in my statutes, and ye shall keep my judgments, and do them.

Ezekiel 36:26,27

God promises to restore us not only physically, but also spiritually. This restoration involves giving us a new heart as tender as flesh so that we will respond to God's Word. Also, God will put His Holy Spirit in us. Apart from the indwelling of the Holy Spirit, it is impossible for a person to have true life and to follow God's ways. It is essential that we remain open to the voice and guidance of the Holy Spirit.

[Not in your own strength] for it is God Who is all the while effectually at work in you — energizing and creating in you the power and desire — both to will and to work for His good pleasure and satisfaction and delight.

Philippians 2:13 Amp

God's grace is at work in His children to produce in them both the desire and power to do His will. However, God's work is not one of compulsion or irresistible force. The work of grace within us is always dependent on our faithfulness and cooperation.

As we yield our lives to the Holy Spirit within us, and as we study and meditate continually in God's Word, we will do much more than memorize verses of scripture. We will do exactly what God's Word tells us to do and, as a result, our Father will bless us in everything that we do.

But if anyone keeps looking steadily into God's law for free men, he will not only remember it but he will do what it says, and God will greatly bless him in everything he does.

James 1:25 TLB

This law is the will of God internalized in our hearts by the indwelling Holy Spirit. Through faith in Christ we receive not only mercy and forgiveness, but also the power and freedom to obey God's law. The Apostle James called obedience "the law for free men," because the believer desires to do God's will. The NIV calls it "the perfect law that gives freedom."

Obedience Brings Freedom

It must never be viewed as a freedom to violate Christ's commands, however, but rather as the freedom and power to obey them. Once Jesus was surrounded by great crowds of people when His disciples told Him that His mother and His brothers were waiting to see Him but could not get to Him because of the tremendous crowds.

Jesus replied, . . . **My mother and my brethren are these which hear the word of God, and do it** (Luke 8:21).

Only those who hear and obey the Word of God are personally related to Jesus and are a part of God's family. Faith without obedience is not an option.

Is Jesus Christ your "big brother"? He has clearly told us that He expects His brothers (and sisters) on earth to do what God's Word tells us to do. There is no other way to prosper under God's laws of prosperity and success.

> **. . . Keep the law of the Lord thy God. Then shalt thou prosper, if thou takest heed to fulfil the statutes . . . .**
> **1 Chronicles 22:12,13**

We can enjoy prosperity on this troubled earth, if we will do what our Father tells us to do and live as His Word tells us to live: **If they obey and serve him, they shall spend their days in prosperity, and their years in pleasures** (Job 36:11). Again and again, God's Word ties the words *prosper* and *prosperity* to the Word *do*. If we *do* what God's Word tells us, we will *prosper* at everything we do and in every direction that we turn.

And keep the charge of the Lord thy God, to walk in his ways, to keep His statutes, and his command- ments, and his judgment, and his testimonies, as it is written in the law of Moses, that thou mayest prosper in all that thou doest, and whithersoever thou turnest thy self.

1 Kings 2:3

If we will obey His instructions, our Father will enable us to *eat the good of the land*, to enjoy the best this world has to offer. (Isa. 1:19). Would you like to live a long life, a good, full, peaceful, complete life? God's Word tells us exactly how to do this:

My son, forget not my law; but let thine heart keep my commandments: For length of days, and long life, and peace, shall they add to thee.

Proverbs 3:1,2

Generally speaking, obeying God and living by His holy principles will result in better health, a longer life, and a happier and more prosperous life. Let us look closely at three words in Proverbs 3:2: 1) length of days, 2) long life, and 3) peace.

When I first looked at these words, I thought they meant long life. However, that is not true, because the words "and long life" immediately follow. Then I realized Solomon meant that, if we obey God's Word, He will "lengthen our *days*"; in other words, we will be able to get a lot more done each day.

This is exactly what has happened in my life. For the past 20 years I have spent great amounts of time studying and meditating in God's Word and doing my best to live my life as His Word tells me. During that time, I have seen amazing changes in my time control.

I am doing much more today than I ever did before, yet I do it with a lot more ease and much better overall balance in my life than ever before. Even though my daily schedule is full, I am able to get everything done that needs to be done and still enjoy good balance in my life in the areas of family time, recreational time, exercise, and so forth. It is true the Lord will bless us with "longer," or fuller days to the degree we are obedient to His Word.

God's Word tells us that we can actually put ourselves in a position where His blessing will "come on" us and "overtake" us. We do not have to chase after God's blessings! His Word says that they will pursue us and "overtake" us.

And it shall come to pass, if thou shalt hearken diligently unto the voice of the Lord thy God, to observe and to do all his commandments which I command thee this day, that the Lord thy God will set thee on high above all nations of the earth: And all these blessing shall come on thee, and overtake thee, if thou shalt hearken unto the voice of the Lord thy God.

Deuteronomy 28:1-2

The New Testament writers often refer to the contents of Deuteronomy. Jesus also quoted from that book when He was tempted by Satan and as He taught about our relationship with God embodied in "the first and greatest commandment." (Matt. 22:38.) How beautifully all of this comes together!

Our Father tells us that He wants us to "hearken diligently" to His voice in order to find out how He wants us to live our lives. Then He tells us we need to do exactly what His Word tells us to do. If we do this, He says that He will set us on high.

He will place us in a realm of spiritual knowledge that will put us above the way most people on earth live their lives. If we do what our Father's Word tells us to do, His blessing will come after us and overtake us. It is up to us. God has given all of us freedom of choice.

He has given us His laws of prosperity, which I have outlined in specific detail in this book. If we follow them, we will prosper in every area. If we insist on living our lives in our own way, then we must be willing to pay the penalty for disobedience. Many Christians say they know God's laws, but their words and actions show they do not.

We will be tested constantly in this life, and our final results will be based, not on what we think we know, but on what we actually say and do during these tests of life. One way God tests us is in the handling of money. He can clearly see how we observe His instruction by what each of us does in an area very important to all of us — our finances.

The rest of this book will outline in detail the various tests all of us must pass in regard to the way that we handle our finances. We are told exactly what our Father wants us to do with our money. If we follow every one of these instructions, we will prosper in all areas of our lives regardless of the world's economic situation.

12

The Foundation of Prosperity: Sowing and Reaping

Give, and it shall be given unto you; good measure, pressed down, and shaken together, and running over, shall men give into your bosom. For with the same measure ye mete withal it shall be measured to you again.

Luke 6:38

The remaining chapters in this book will be based upon one Biblical principle: *God's law of sowing and reaping.* This law went into effect when God created the earth and will never cease to be operative as long as the earth lasts: **While the earth remaineth, seedtime and harvest, and cold and heat, and summer and winter, and day and night shall not cease** (Gen. 8:22).

Jesus told us every area in the kingdom of God is based upon the principles of sowing and reaping. We plant seeds in the ground, and they sprout and grow even though we cannot understand how all of this works.

And He said, So is the kingdom of God, as if a man should cast seed into the ground; And should sleep,

101

and rise, night and day, and the seed should spring and grow up, he knoweth not how.
Mark 4:26,27

We know how God's laws of sowing and reaping work in the natural realm, in the area of planting seeds for flowers, fruits, and vegetables. What many people do not know is that the same law of sowing and reaping works in other areas of our lives. The basic verse on sowing and reaping simply tells us: **. . . Whatsoever a man soweth, that shall he also reap** (Gal. 6:7).

If we want corn, we have to plant corn seeds.

If we want carrots, we have to plant carrot seeds.

If we want tomatoes, we have to plant tomato seeds.

This is very obvious. However, God's law of sowing and reaping go far beyond the agricultural realm. It applies to every area of our lives. For example, consider a husband who believes his wife does not love him enough. How can he receive more love from her?

Should he demand that she love him more?

Should he insist on it?

Should he try to force her to show more love?

If we want to "reap" anything, God's Word tells us that we have to "sow" that kind of seed. "Like begets like." (Gen. 1:24,25.) What kinds of seeds should we sow if we want more love? Jesus gave us the answer in "the Golden Rule": **Therefore all things whatsoever ye would that men should do to you, do ye even so to them: for this is the law and the prophets** (Matt. 7:12).

If we want to receive more love, we first of all must plant seeds of love ourselves. We will reap exactly what we sow: **A man that hath friends must shew himself friendly . . .** (Prov. 18:24). This principle works in the area of faith also, because Jesus compared faith to a "seed": **. . . If ye have faith as a grain of mustard seed . . .** (Matt. 17:20).

Just what is this faith of which Jesus spoke?

• True faith is an effective faith that produces results: It will move mountains. (Matt. 17:20.)

• True faith is not a belief in *faith* as a force of power, but it is a faith in *God* — not a faith in one's faith.

• True faith is a work of God within the hearts of Christians. It involves an awareness divinely imparted to our hearts that our prayers are answered. It is created within us by the Holy Spirit; we cannot produce it in our own minds.

• True faith is a gift imparted to us by Christ, therefore, it is important to draw near to Christ and His Word and to deepen our commitment to, and confidence in, Him. We are dependent on Him for everything: **. . . For without me ye can do nothing** (John 15:5). In other words, we must seek Christ as the author and perfecter of our faith. His close presence and our obedience to His Word are the source and the secret of faith.

• True faith is under God's control. Faith is given on the basis of His love, wisdom, grace, and kingdom purpose. It is given to accomplish His will and to express His love for us. If we sow enough seeds of faith and patiently wait for our "crop" to come in, we will receive a harvest.

No one wants to reap a poor harvest, but God's laws of sowing and reaping work both ways. The same ground that births a beautiful rose also will produce ugly weeds. Many of us have sown seeds of anger, criticism, or unforgiveness. As a result, other people have been angry, irritable, and critical towards us. Jesus made it easy to determine what kind of seeds you have been sowing: **Wherefore by their fruits ye shall know them** (Matt. 7:20).

If we have planted seeds of love, faith, and kindness, we can tell this by the results — the fruit we are receiving in our lives. On the other hand, if we have been planting the other kind of seeds, we can tell this by the negative results in our lives: **... As thou hast done, it shall be done unto thee: thy reward shall return upon thine own head** (Obad. 1:15).

Like Begets Like

How could God's laws of sowing and reaping be any clearer? Whatever we want to receive more of, we need to sow more of that very thing. All of us have seen how God's laws of sowing and reaping apply to seeds planted in the ground. We also can see how these same laws apply to love, kindness, anger, criticism, and other intangible areas.

However, many Christians fail to realize these very same laws of sowing and reaping apply to finances. *If we want to reap a harvest of money, we must sow seeds of money.* God's laws of sowing and reaping work in the financial realm just as they do in agriculture and in human relations.

We should never hesitate to do good things with any attributes that we possess. God's Word tells us that whatever good thing we do for others, he will give back to us: **... Whatsoever good thing any man doeth, the same shall he receive of the Lord ...** (Eph. 6:8). Whenever we give our abilities, our love, our kindness, or our money, what we are really giving is a portion of ourselves.

When we give of ourselves, this plants a seed which gives our Father the "channel" He needs in order to give back to us under His fair and impartial laws of sowing and reaping. God's Word contains some facts that clearly show how His laws of sowing and reaping apply to our finances.

Let us start with the one verse of scripture that perfectly describes the financial prosperity that our Father has available for those who follow His laws of prosperity and success. I have used *The Amplified Bible* version of this verse, because I believe it does an excellent job of showing the total prosperity available, if we follow God's laws of prosperity.

> **And God is able to make all grace (every favor and earthly blessing) come to you in abundance, so that you may always and under all circumstances and whatever the need, be self-sufficient — possessing enough to require no aid or support and furnished in abundance for every good work and charitable donation.**
>
> **2 Corinthians 9:8**

Believers who give what they can to help those in need will find God's grace provides a sufficiency for their own needs, and more, so that they abound in every good work. Is this not magnificent? Our Father is able to abundantly provide every blessing in our lives so that, no matter what happens, every need can be met with enough left for every charitable donation we are led to give.

God's Word not only tells us this type of prosperity is available, but that it is *always* available to us under all circumstances. In other words, no matter what the world's economy is doing, our Father is able to provide abundantly for us. Look at 2 Corinthians 9:8 in the *King James Version*.

> **And God is able to make all grace abound toward you; that ye, always having all sufficiency in all things, may abound to every good work.**

I have never seen a verse with more positive statements. It is full of words such as *all, always, every,* and *abound* (which comes from the same root Greek word translated *abundance*). How can God's Word be any clearer? How much promise can be contained in one short verse of scripture? I never cease to be thrilled atthe strong, powerful, positive words in this verse.

105

However, there is one key word at the start of the verse that must be discussed and that is *able*.

We are not told that God will always provide all of this for us. This is not automatic for all Christians. If it were, we would never see any Christians with financial problems. This verse says God is "able" to provide great prosperity for us, but it does not say that He will.

What changes "God is able" to *God will*? Do you know the answer? It is not hard to find. All we need is to read the two verses immediately preceding the beautiful promises of verse 8. The *King James Version* shows this very clearly. Look at all three verses together to see the whole picture.

> **But this I say, he which soweth sparingly shall reap also sparingly; and he which soweth bountifully shall reap also bountifully. Every man according as he purposeth in his heart, so let him give; not grudgingly or of necessity: for God loveth a cheerful giver. And God is *able* to make all grace abound toward you: that ye, always having all sufficiency in all things, may abound to every good work.**
>
> **2 Corinthians 9:6-8**

Christians can give either generously or sparingly; God will reward them accordingly. Giving is not a loss, but a form of saving; it results in substantial benefits for those who give. He is not speaking primarily of the *quantity* given, but of the *quality* of our heart's desires and motives.

The poor widow gave little, but God considered it much because of the proportion she gave and her complete dedication. (Luke 21:2.)

How do we obtain "all sufficiency in all things"? We obtain this by sowing bountifully — by sowing many financial seeds as a result of giving cheerfully to the Lord. When we do this, God's Word says we will reap bountifully.

If we sow sparingly, we will reap a modest harvest. God wants us to sow seeds by giving money for our benefit, not His! God does not need our money. He already owns the whole world and everything in it.

Heaven is also His — an abundant place where people walk on streets of pure gold. (Rev. 21:21.) Our Father wants us to give in order to provide Him with seeds to multiply back to us. God gives us seeds to sow, not to "store up" or to hang on to. God does not multiply the seeds we retain. He only multiplies the seeds we sow.

God's Economy Is Opposite to the World's

The world says we should cling tightly to our money so we will not run out. God's laws of prosperity tell us our dollars are seeds which we should plant so He can give us a harvest. Seeds are not worth anything in agriculture until they are planted. The same is true in the financial realm.

Jesus Christ is a perfect example of God's laws of sowing and reaping. When Jesus gave His life on the cross, He planted the greatest seed in the history of mankind. God "sowed" by giving His only Son, and Jesus "sowed" by giving His life. They will reap an ultimate harvest of hundreds of millions of people into their Family — all those who ever have and ever will accept Jesus Christ as Lord and Savior. Jesus explained this:

> **"I must fall and die like a kernel of wheat that falls into the furrows of the earth. Unless I die I will be alone — a single seed. But my death will produce many new wheat kernels — a plentiful harvest of new lives."**
>
> **John 12:24** TLB

The only way any seed can grow is to be buried in the ground and die. This is true in agriculture, true in the death of Jesus Christ, and true in the life of every Christian. Before any of us can enter into God's family, we must "die" to the concept that we can provide our own eternal life in heaven.

Instead, we have to trust Jesus for this. This same principle applies to our finances. Before we can reap a financial harvest, our money must die. We must give it up and die to self. We must sow it as we sow seeds, letting go of it and planting it. We must trust our Father to take these financial seeds and use them to produce the necessary harvest in our lives.

Some people say, "I would like to give, but I do not have anything to give."

This is not true. God will give all of us a seed to start with and, as we sow this one seed, He will multiply it so that we will always have seeds to sow: **And [God] Who provides seed for the sower and bread for eating will also provide and multiply your [resources for] sowing . . .** (2 Cor. 9:10 Amp).

Each of us has to start from wherever we are financially. We need to take whatever we have to sow, and sow it with faith. We need to trust God to multiply this and return what we have sown and provide for our needs with enough left over to sow again.

All over the world people are trying to reap financial harvests without planting financial seeds. No one would think of going out in the summer to get some tomatoes if they had not planted tomatoes in the spring. But this is exactly what many people are doing with their finances! We cannot expect to withdraw from a heavenly bank account if we have not put deposits into it. I ask each reader three questions:

1. Do you have financial problems?

2. If you do, what sort of financial seeds have you sown?

3. Have you sown sparingly, or have you sown bountifully? (2 Cor. 9:6.)

It is possible to give away and become richer! It is also possible to hold on too tightly and lose everything. Yes, the liberal man shall be rich! By watering others, he waters himself.

Proverbs 11:24,25 TLB

If a farmer wants a large crop, he plants a large number of seeds. No farmer would expect a large crop if he planted only a few seeds. Why should we think a finanical harvest operates any differently?

If we need to receive a large financial harvest, why would we plant a few (or no) seeds? This does not make sense. When we have financial problems, we can give our way out of these problems!

The unrenewed mind cannot understand this, but it is true. If we refuse to give freely, we are heading in the opposite direction from God. We are pulling against Him instead of with Him. If we want God to multiply back to us, we must give Him the seeds to multiply. If we need to receive a large financial harvest, we need to plant a large number of financial seeds.

When I first realized this great truth, I was living in poverty and want. Nevertheless, I started sowing financial seeds. I sowed bountifully. Day after day I would instruct my wife, Sue, to send contributions to my church and various ministries. The worse our finances got, the more checks we sent.

The results have been amazing. Over and over during these past years, whenever we have had financial problems, we have increased our giving and every time — without fail — the money we needed has come in. Sometimes we have had to be very patient, but it has always come.

We cannot outgive God! However, we need to give Him a channel by which He can give to us. That channel is the seeds we plant through giving.

Don't Eat Your Seeds

Also, we should not "eat" all of our harvest. No farmer would do this, and neither should we. We should not use up all of our income, but continuously "replant" from our income. As God gives us a harvest, we should plow it back again and again. If we resist the temptation of "eating" the surplus, and continually sow seeds, we are on our way to prosperity.

When the Lord starts to multiply back to us, we should take out what we need and sow abundantly from the remainder, resisting greed. Any Christian who will do this cheerfully will find he or she will always be provided for abundantly with plenty left over to continue to give to every good work. (1 Cor. 9:8.)

Believers who give what they can to help those in need will find that God's grace provides a sufficiency for their own needs, and even more, that they abound in every good work. I believe God wants His children to prosper financially for two reasons:

1. I believe our economy is going to change tremendously during the next several years. World financial principles that have worked for many years are not going to work any longer. It is imperative for God's children to learn and apply His laws of financial prosperity during the difficult economic years ahead of us.

2. I believe we must learn and apply God's laws of prosperity in order to fulfill the Great Commission given to us by our Lord Jesus Christ: **Go ye into all the world, and preach the gospel to every creature** (Mark 16:15). He also said: **And this gospel of the kingdom shall be preached in all the world for a witness unto all nations; and then shall the end come** (Matt. 24:14).

Christ spoke to the disciples as though everything He predicted could be fulfilled within their generation. Therefore the hope of the New Testament Church was for Jesus' return. The hope of all who believe in Jesus through the ages should be that the end of the age will occur in their generation.

We must live in a tension between the imminence of Christ's coming and the fact that Christ has commanded us to keep on spreading the gospel. This commission is for the entire church. If we are not personally called to be a missionary, our responsibility is to provide financial support for those who do. More than two billion people have never heard the gospel of Jesus.

All Christians share the responsibility of seeing that these people are given the same opportunity for eternal salvation and Christian growth that we have had. Hundreds of billions of dollars will be needed to finance this great revival of the Holy Spirit, already beginning to spread all over the world. Hundreds of thousands of additional missionaries will be needed.

Worldwide revival will be paid for by millions of Christians who are willing to pay the price of learning and applying God's laws of prosperity.

God's laws of sowing and reaping clearly indicate He wants us to reap much more than we sow. As I have pointed out, we can see this by looking at all the seeds inside watermelons, oranges, apples and grapefruits.

Obviously, God gives us many more seeds than we need. Our Father knows no limits. If any limits are set, *we set them* — not God. He wants us to stretch our faith, then stretch it more and more and more. As we release our faith again and again and again, He will continually give us an increase of the money that we sow back into His kingdom.

As our Father keeps giving us an increase, we need to keep plowing it back into His kingdom. He gives us the increase; we plant the increase. He gives us more increase; we plant more increase. On and on it goes. God does not want us to stop. I am convinced that, in these last days before Jesus returns, our Father wants large numbers of Christians all over the world to fully grasp and utilize His laws of sowing and reaping.

If we fully understand these laws and constantly apply them, the Lord will use us as a channel. Not only will He meet all our needs regardless of what is happening in the world, but large amounts of money will flow through our hands, because He knows we will reinvest this money in His Kingdom.

Are you one of those whom our Father wants to sow and reap over and over again, always sowing more, always reaping more, and constantly planting the increase back into His kingdom? It is awesome to comprehend what can be done through a believing Christian who fully understands and fully applies God's laws of sowing and reaping.

13
Tithing: The Key to the Bank of Heaven

Bring ye all the tithes into the storehouse ... and prove me now herewith, saith the Lord of hosts, if I will not open you the windows of heaven, and pour you out a blessing, that there shall not be room enough to receive it.

Malachi 3:10

God's great laws of sowing and reaping can be put into application through tithing. The word *tithe* means "one-tenth," so tithing to God means giving a minimum of 10 percent of our income to God. Today, we refer to tithing in terms of income. In Bible times, tithing meant giving the first fruits of crops, produce, cattle, and so forth; that was their income.

Why should Christians today tithe? God's Word tells us exactly why we should tithe: to remind us to put God first in everything in our lives and to have a part in the ministry of expanding the Kingdom of God.

An old saying is very true: If God does not have authority over your pocketbook, He really has no authority over you.

As we have seen, God's laws of prosperity and success make God first while the world's system of prosperity puts money first. Tithing is one of God's tests that shows clearly whether we really do keep Him first.

Here are four basic verses of scripture on the subject of tithing:

> **Will a man rob God? Yet ye have robbed me. But ye say, wherein have we robbed thee? In tithes and offerings. Ye are cursed with a curse: for ye have robbed me, even this whole nation. Bring ye all the tithes into the storehouse, that there may be meat in mine house, and prove me now herewith, saith the Lord of hosts, if I will not open you the windows of heaven, and pour you out a blessing that there shall not be room enough to receive it. And I will rebuke the devourer for your sakes, and he shall not destroy the fruits of your ground; neither shall your vine cast her fruit before the time in the field, saith the Lord of hosts.**
>
> **Malachi 3:8-11**

These four verses of scripture have caused a great deal of controversy among Christians. If those verses do apply to Christians, those who do not tithe at least 10 percent of their income are thieves, just as God called the Jews. Some Christians, however, say tithing is part of the Jewish law and Christians are not under that law. What is the truth?

Are we required to tithe or not? It is my personal belief that it is impossible for Christians to prosper under God's system without tithing. However, we should not tithe legalistically (because we have to), but because we know tithing is part of God's overall principles of sowing and reaping.

Abraham instituted the tithe at least 400 years before the Jewish (Mosaic) law went into effect. Genesis 14:19-20 tells us that Abraham was a tither and that he was blessed by God. Abraham did not tithe because he had to. There was no "Mosaic law" in his day. He tithed because he loved the Lord and

114

because he knew 10 percent of his income belonged to the Lord.

I believe we should tithe because, through Jesus Christ, we are heirs of Abraham. (Gal. 3:29.) Jesus told the Pharisees they were not truly "Abraham's children" (although they were natural-born descendants of the tribe of Judah) *unless* they followed Abraham's ways. I believe the same is true of believers today. True Spirit-born children of Abraham will follow His example and ways:

> . . . **Jesus said, If you were truly Abraham's children, then you would do the works of Abraham — you would follow his example, do as Abraham did.**
>
> **John 8:39 Amp**

I believe tithing is every bit as much a New Testament principle as an Old Testament principle. In Matthew 23:23, Jesus castigated the Pharisees because they tithed legalistically, not out of a heart toward God. Jesus then said that, yes, they should tithe, but not leave the other things undone:

> **"Yes, woe upon you, Pharisees, and you other religious leaders — hypocrites! For you tithe down to the last mint leaf in your garden, but ignore the important things — justice and mercy and faith. Yes, you should tithe, but you should not leave the more important things undone."**
>
> **Matthew 23:23 TLB**

Tithing Was Never "Done Away With"

Jesus apparently accepted the fact that tithing was incumbent on God's people. How can any of us honestly say that God is first in every area of our lives when we fail to give Him at least the first 10 percent of our money? We should tithe first and pay our bills from the remainder.

Too many people do just the opposite, then wonder why they do not prosper. They do not prosper because they fail to follow God's laws of prosperity and success! God does not want our leftovers — whatever remains after all our bills are paid. He wants the first fruits — the first 10 percent. When we do this on a continuing basis, God will provide abundantly for us.

> **Honour the Lord with thy substance, and with the firstfruits of all thine increase: So shall thy barns be filled with plenty, and thy presses shall burst out with new wine.**
>
> **Proverbs 3:9,10**

The Israelites brought the first portion of their harvest to the Lord to acknowledge that He was owner of the land, and they were only stewards. We also should give God the first fruits of our income to honor Him as Lord of our lives and possessions. God will then open the way to pour out His blessing on us.

In the days of the Early Church, the apostles continued the practice of tithing:

> **Upon the first day of the week let every one of you lay by him in store, as God hath prospered him . . . .**
>
> **1 Corinthians 16:2**

Our Father wants us to put Him first and then trust Him to meet all of our needs and then some. Tithing is an act of faith. It takes faith to give money "off the top," but not much faith to give God what is left. When we willingly tithe, this brings us into the proper financial relationship with Him.

When we tithe, meditate day and night in His Word, confess God's Word with our mouths, and do what it says, we come into partnership with God. We align ourselves with God's laws of prosperity. He becomes our senior partner. We have His wisdom and direction in every area of our finances.

He is the senior partner, but He only asks for a minimum of 10 percent of the income of the partnership and allows us to keep 90 percent. This is one of the greatest offers God ever made to His children! Yet many of us try to keep 95 percent, or more!

Is it fair to withhold our senior partner's money from Him? What partnership could ever flourish if the senior partner only asked for a small percentage of the profit, and then the junior partner withheld some of even that small amount? This is exactly what many of us do.

God is the greatest financial genius of all time. He always has been and always will be. When we tithe and follow His other laws of prosperity, we receive His wisdom in our finances and in every area of our lives, because His laws of prosperity apply to much more than just our finances.

When you tithe and follow God's other laws of prosperity, you will find that 90 percent will do more than 100 percent used to do. I can tell you, after several years of practical experience, that 90 percent of our income with the blessing of God goes a lot farther than 100 percent without His blessing.

Week after week people have given me testimonies of blessings received as a result of tithing. The cumulative effect of all of these months of testimony is absolutely awesome.

One of the most difficult things for many people to give up is their money. Our Father knows this. This is exactly why His laws of prosperity require us to release our money in order to receive financial blessing from him. Too many Christians are looking for God to open the windows of heaven and bless them financially when they are proudly putting $10 in the collection plate each Sunday morning. God's laws do not work this way. We cannot expect God to fulfill the last part of Malachi 3:10 until we do the first part.

The unrenewed, carnal mind simply cannot grasp these concepts of tithing and thinks, "If I cannot pay my bills with the money I have now, how can I possibly pay them if I give up an additional 10 percent of my income?"

That sounds logical, according to the world's logic; however, as we have seen in Scripture, God's ways are much higher than man's ways. (Isa. 55:8,9.) God's thoughts and ways are not those of the natural person. Human minds and hearts can be renewed and transformed by seeking Him; then our thoughts and ways will begin to conform to His. Our greatest desire should be to live so in conformity to Jesus that everything we do pleases God. We do this by abiding in His Word and responding to the Holy Spirit's leading.

Tithing Puts God First

When we tithe, we honor God by putting Him first. His Word says He will honor us in return, **. . . them that honour me I will honour . . .** (1 Sam. 2:30). In Malachi 3:10, God challenges us to *prove* Him. This is the only place in the Bible where God gives us a challenge to *prove* Him.

Why not *prove* God? Why not tithe willingly and cheerfully for a reasonable period of time and see for yourself if God will bless you as His Word says?

Faith is the spiritual power that opens the windows of heaven in every area of our lives. Why would anyone even want to argue whether tithing is or is not "under the law" when God's Word tells us that, if we tithe properly, He will open the windows of heaven and pour out a blessing we do not have room to receive? (Mal. 3:10.)

If we really believe that God will pour out a great blessing, we certainly should not try to get out of tithing! We should be eager to tithe! Is there any reader who would not like God to open up the windows of heaven and pour out such blessings there will not be room to receive them?

The fact is: the 10 percent tithe is only a starting point. It is not a maximum. Over and above the tithe, we can choose to give additional offerings. Giving the tithe guarantees that all of our needs will be met — but Scripture shows us that voluntary offerings over and above the tithe open "the windows of heaven" for tremendous blessings to be poured out.

There is no way anyone should ever expect to reap a bountiful harvest without first of all sowing seeds bountifully. However, the financial offering of most Christians cannot be called "bountiful" by any stretch of the imagination. As this is written, the latest Gallup poll shows that the average American gives a pitiful $250 a year to churches and other religious organizations! Obviously, many Americans are robbing God and, as a result, they are robbing themselves!

Malachi 3:8 tells us that we can rob God not only in our tithe, but also in our offerings. How are we robbing Him? I believe we are robbing Him by failing to open the windows of heaven wide enough so He can really pour out blessings upon us!

How many readers of this book have tithed exactly 10 percent and can say that God has poured out so many blessings they cannot contain them? I know many people who tithe and are blessed, but they are not coming close to getting so many blessings there is not enough room to receive them.

I challenge you to seek out Christians who have voluntarily increased their tithes and offerings from 10 percent to 15 percent, 20 percent, 25 percent or even more of their income and ask *them* if God has not poured out His blessings just as He said he would.

I would like to give you a personal example. I am a self-employed businessman with 30 sales representatives representing my firm. Let me tell you how two of them have applied the preceding principles. Most of my sales representatives are Christians, and most of them tithe about 10 percent of their income. However, two young men (average age 35), who were not Christians when they joined my firm, have since given their lives to Jesus Christ. In due time, each of these men started to tithe.

Then, they started to give offerings over the tithe. These two now give tithes and offerings far in excess of 10 percent. Are they broke? Has this caused hardships? Not in the least — quite the contrary. Both have been able to purchase beautiful homes since they became Christians. Their incomes have increased by an average of almost 300 percent in the few short years since they started increasing their tithes and offerings.

Start with 10 percent. Prove to yourself that 90 percent will go as far or farther than 100 percent used to, but do not stop there! God will pour out more blessings if you plant more seeds. At this point, some readers may be concerned because they are on fixed incomes or a fixed salary. A definite way to increase income is to tithe based on what you would *like* to earn rather than what you now earn.

Do not limit God because of your doubts as to whether or not your employer will increase your income. Our Father has many ways to increase our incomes if we release our faith and do not block Him through doubt and unbelief. He might choose to increase your income through a pay raise or a bonus from your present employer, or through an entirely different source.

14

Tithing "Primes the Pump"

But this I say, He which soweth sparingly shall reap also sparingly; and he which soweth bountifully shall reap also bountifully.

2 Corinthians 9:6

Do you honestly believe God will see to it that you reap bountifully if you sow bountifully? Then why would you have any concern whatever about going well past 10 percent? What Christian with a renewed mind would willingly stop at that level, knowing God will bless more if more is given? Tithing merely "primes the pump." The real blessings of God pour out in proportion to the offerings we cheerfully give above our tithes.

Do not consume the excess; do not "eat your seeds"; do not store or hoard your seeds. Keep plowing them back until you are able to live well on 80 percent of your income, for example. People who steadily increase their offerings will be surprised how easy this becomes. It was much easier for me to give 15 percent than it was to tithe 10 percent, and easier to give 20 percent than it was to give 15 percent.

I have increased my tithes and offerings to the point where I now pay more income tax each year than my total yearly earnings were when I started tithing — and I believe this is just the start. My goal is to give God 85 to 90 percent of my income. Constant yearly increases in my tithes and offering will result in an income to meet all my needs on 5 to 10 percent of the total.

God's blessings do not stop here. They go one step farther. After God told of the blessings He would pour out, He said, **And I will rebuke the devourer for your sakes** (Mal. 3:11). The devourer is Satan. If we give freely of our tithes and offerings, God will rebuke the devourer so **he shall not destroy the fruits of your ground**.

God was speaking to farmers, but this same principle applies to those of any occupation. Whatever our line of work, God promises to rebuke Satan so he cannot destroy the blessings God gives us as a result of our tithes and offerings. Whatever method Satan uses to try to steal these blessings will be rebuked by God Himself.

Malachi 3:11 is the only place in the Bible where God said He would rebuke the devil for us. Jesus gave us the authority to do this ourselves (Luke 10:19), but when it comes to receiving blessings from our tithes and offerings, God Himself makes certain Satan does not steal our blessings. Imagine how Satan must feel when God Himself stands in his way!

How can any of us fail to give liberally if we fully understand what Malachi 3:10-11 says that God will do in return? Christian businessmen who give freely of their tithes and offerings will find they prosper regardless of what is going on in the world's economy.

The principles of giving tithes and offerings not only apply to individuals, but apply to us collectively as members of a particular church. If you know of a vibrant growing church, check it out for yourself. I guarantee all or most of its members give freely of their tithes and offerings.

Growth and tithing go hand in hand, individually and collectively. God gives every church enough people to act as a "seed." These people then have to do their part. They need to learn God's laws and apply them in their lives. If they do this properly, they will prosper and grow as individuals and their church will prosper and grow as we will.

If churches would teach God's laws of prosperity and success, and if members of congregations would learn and apply them in their lives, fund-raising dinners, rummage sales, and similar fund-raising devices would eventually disappear. God would pour out so many financial blessings on these churches they would not be able to receive them!

The same principles apply to nations. I believe God blesses entire countries in the same way He blesses individuals and groups of individuals. I believe the United States has been blessed so abundantly, because a far greater percentage of its people have tithed than in any other country. Also, I believe many of the blessings of the Untied States have been possible because, in the past, we had liberal tax deductions for tithes and offerings.

Children should be taught to give tithes and offerings from their allowances and to trust God to meet their needs in return. I also believe the local church should be the center of all this teaching as well as the recipient of our tithes. Malachi 3:10 says, **Bring ye all the tithes into the storehouse**. The "storehouse" is where we are spiritually fed.

If the local church is doing its job properly, this is where its members are fed spiritually each week — on Sunday mornings, in Bible study classes, in home fellowship groups, and often, in Christian schools. It is our obligation to give first to the local teacher.

Let him who receives instructions in the Word [of God] share all good things with his teacher — contributing to his support.

Galatians 6:6 Amp

It is the duty of all who are taught God's Word to help provide material support for those who instruct. Those worthy of support include faithful pastors, teachers, evangelists, or missionaries. To refuse to give support when possible is to sow selfishness and reap destruction. To give to those who minister in the Word is part of doing good to those in the family of believers. At the proper time we will reap both reward and eternal life.

Offerings Are To Go Where the Lord Leads

Tithes should go to the local church, but offerings go where the Lord leads. Also, the local church should give tithes and offerings on everything it receives — to needy individuals within the church, to missionaries, and other ministries the pastor, elders, and deacons feel led to give. We have followed this procedure in our church, and the Lord has blessed us abundantly as a result.

I am often asked if people who are seriously in debt should pay tithes. My answer is a resounding *yes!* Worldly logic says the debtor cannot afford to tithe. Spiritual truth says the primary way to escape from the bondage of debt is to pay God's money first and trust Him to meet our needs.

I did this when I was so deeply in debt I had to "reach up to touch bottom." This, plus meditating day and night on God's laws of prosperity, speaking them with my mouth and acting on them in my life, got me out of debt! These same principles will get anyone out of debt who follows them exactly and sticks with them long enough for God to bring the harvest.

124

God does not put us in financial prison. We put ourselves there! God can and will get us out if we follow His laws of prosperity properly. Many people have come to me for financial counseling, and I have seen these principles work in their lives. People seriously in debt are desperate. They think about their debts all the time. Their debts literally consume them. I know what they are going through. I have been there.

Step by step I take them through God's laws of prosperity, trying to get their eyes off the problem and onto the solution. Over and over people tell me exactly what they owe, when the money is due, and what will happen to them if they do not pay. Over and over I reply with promises from the Bible. I urge them to spend at least as much time focusing on solutions in God's Word as on every detail of bondage in which they find themselves.

God's laws of prosperity work. If people are not so bound up with fear as a result of their financial problems that they reject the teachings of God, these teachings will show them the way out of their financial prison. In the world, people study *The Wall Street Journal* and stock market tips to decide how to handle their money. This is fine for man's system of prosperity, but God's system is better!

Tithes and offerings are better than any investment this world has ever seen. God's laws of tithing and giving are more precise and exact than the world's laws of finance. If we pay the price of following God's laws of prosperity, no financial problem on earth will be able to defeat us.

Here is a "short cut" to overcoming the fear of tithing and entering into the land of abundance. Repeat these affirmations to yourself, one each day, until you *believe* the scriptures on which they are based.

Monday: God has not given me a spirit of fear, but of power, and of love, and of a sound mind. (2 Tim. 1:7.)

Tuesday: I honor the Lord with my substance, and with the firstfruits of all my increase: so shall my barns be filled with plenty, and my presses burst out with new wine. (Prov. 3:9.)

Wednesday: God is able to make all grace abound toward me, so that I, having all sufficiency in all things, do abound to every good work. (2 Cor. 9:8.)

Thursday: Since I am *willing and obedient*, I do eat of the good of the land. (Isa. 1:9.)

Friday: I give, and it is given unto me: good measure, pressed down, shaken together, and running over do men give unto my bosom. For with the same measure that I give, it is measured to me again. (Luke 6:38.)

Saturday: Because I sow bountifully, so also do I reap bountifully. I purpose to give what I give cheerfully, for I please the heavenly Father when I give cheerfully. (2 Cor. 9:6.)

15
Can You Outgive God?

Honor the Lord by giving Him the first part of all your income, and he will fill your barns with wheat and barley and overflow your wine vats with the finest wines.

Proverbs 3:9,10 TLB

Sowing and reaping, tithing and giving overlap in some areas, but in each area there is a wealth of scripture not covered in the other areas. For example, the Word teaches that all giving should be based upon love.

If I gave everything I have to poor people, and if I were buried alive for preaching the Gospel but didn't love others, it would be of no value whatever.

1 Corinthians 13:3 TLB

Some people learn part of God's laws of prosperity and give in a calculating manner, anticipating something in return. This will not work! Giving without love is *of no value whatsoever*. No matter what we give, if our gift is not based upon love, it is worth nothing.

Love is the key to giving, and only love opens the channels for our loving Father to give back to us. Our Father has given us

127

very definite laws for giving and receiving. Let us start with the foundation verse of scripture on this and expand from there.

> **Give, and it shall be given unto you; good measure, pressed down, and shaken together, and running over, shall men give into your bosom. For with the same measure ye mete withal it shall be measured to you again.**
>
> **Luke 6:38**

God Himself will measure our giving and in return will give to us. The measure of blessing and reward we receive will be in proportion to our concern for and help given to others. There is a tremendous depth of meaning in this one verse of scripture. This verse starts by simply telling us that if we give, we will receive in return. This ties in exactly with **whatsoever a man soweth, that shall he also reap** (Gal. 6:7).

Giving is a seed and, if we sow it properly, God will see that we receive a harvest. *The Living Bible* paraphrases this part of Luke 6:38 beautifully: **Your gift will return to you in full and overflowing measure, pressed down, shaken together to make room for more, and running over.**

We cannot outgive God! When we give according to God's laws, our gift will come back to us overflowing and running over.

Imagine a large container of oats. Before we receive from these oats they are *pressed down* into the bottom of the container, enabling more oats to be added. Then the oats are *shaken together* to settle down again, enabling still more oats to be added. When this process is completed, the container is filled to overflowing. It is so full oats are *running over* the sides.

This is how God's Word tells us we will receive if we give freely according to His laws of giving. This ties in with Malachi 3:10 which tells us that, if we give tithes and offerings, God will

128

open the windows of heaven and pour out so many blessings we will not have room to receive them. God clearly promises to give back all that we give, and much, much more.

How will God give back to you?

Will He just pour money down from heaven? No, Luke 6:38 tells us that *men* will give unto us.

What does this mean? It means that our Father has arranged it so that His children who follow His laws of giving will receive — from other people. As we give generously to others, our Father will inspire other men and women to give to us. This giving can be in many forms.

• We might receive an especially good deal in business.

• We might buy or sell a home, a car or some other property in a manner that is very favorable to us.

• If we are self-employed, people might be led to do business with us.

• If we are employed, our employer may be led to give us a promotion, a pay raise, or a bonus. Or, we might be offered a new job much better than the one we have.

Those are only a few of the numerous ways our Father can use to cause other men to give to us.

What part do we play in getting other people to give to us? As we have seen, God's Word tells us this is accomplished by constant giving to others. (Matt. 7:12.)

Our Part Is To Give

Whatever we want to reap, we first must sow. This is God's law. We determine exactly how much others give to us. How do we do this? The closing words of Luke 6:38 told us how: **for with the same measure that ye mete withal it shall be measured to you again.**

129

Thus, if we give with a teaspoon, we will receive "teaspoon measure" in return. If we give with a tablespoon, we will receive a "tablespoon measure." If we give by the barrel, we will receive by the barrel. Whatever measure we use to give is exactly what will be used to measure what is given back to us.

The principles of Luke 6:38 apply to every area of our lives — including our finances. Giving money is very important to God, because most of the money and possessions we have were earned by giving of ourselves — our abilities, our energy, and our time. Employment is actually a vehicle we can use to turn ourselves into dollars to be invested in God's work as He leads us to give.

> **... Let him labour, working with his hands the thing which is good, that he may have to give to him that needeth.**
>
> **Ephesians 4:28**

Look at nine words that Jesus Christ said — words that virtually every reader will have heard before: **It is more blessed to give than to receive** (Acts 20:35). Many of us have heard these words many times and think we agree. However, in many cases, I honestly do not believe this is the case. Most people place a lot more emphasis on *getting* than on *giving*. Be completely honest: Do you get more enjoyment from giving than you do from receiving?

Our Father knows us as we really are. I believe that, as He looks at our hearts, He sees many of His children place much more emphasis on receiving than on giving. However, His Word clearly teaches that man was created not to see how much we can get, but to see how much we can give. Untold millions of people have this backwards.

When we are reborn spiritually, our new nature wants to give, but our old nature wants to hang on to what we have.

Jesus would not have said it is more blessed to give than it is to receive if it were not true. Why is it more blessed to give than it is to receive? I can think of four reasons:

1. When we give freely and generously, we put God first, ahead of our own selfish interests. By doing this, we are obeying His Word and this obedience will cause Him to bless us.

2. When we give freely and generously, this shows we trust God. The degree of our giving is a clear indication of our freedom from fear. Freedom from fear is always a blessing.

3. When we give freely and generously, this protects us from the pitfalls of greed and covetousness. Generous giving comes from a humble, loving heart. Greed and selfishness are derived from a prideful "me first" heart which blocks us from the blessings of God: **God resisteth the proud, and giveth grace to the humble** (1 Pet. 5:5).

4. Finally, we are blessed because, the more we give to God, the more this opens the channel for Him to see that we receive abundantly in return.

If we withhold our giving, we are actually withholding the blessing our Father wants to give us. The *receiving* most people want deep down in their hearts actually comes as a result of giving. Another reason Jesus said it is more blessed to give than to receive is literal: by our giving, we *do* receive.

When we grasp these principles, giving really does become a blessing. In fact, we will get to the point where, when we give a little, it hurts, and when we give a great deal, it does not hurt at all! This will sound strange to you if you have not given much, but Christians who have given freely on many occasions will agree to the absolute truth of this statement.

Our Father does not want us to give because we feel it is an obligation. He wants us to give cheerfully:

Every man according as he purposeth in his heart, so let him give; not grudgingly, or of necessity: for God loveth a cheerful giver.

2 Corinthians 9:7

"Grudgingly" is exactly the way many people give to God. They give out of fear, through a sense of duty. They dole out the dollars carefully and begrudge what they do give.

God did not give us His Son grudgingly.

Jesus did not give His life grudgingly on the cross. He gladly paid the debt for every sin ever committed by anyone who ever will live on this earth. None of us could begin to repay Jesus for what He did for us if we had trillions of dollars and gave it all to Him.

Giving Grudgingly Kills the Harvest

It is interesting to study the Greek word translated *cheerful* in 2 Corinthians 9:7. This Greek word is *hilares*, which means "noisy and full of fun and laughter." This is how God wants us to give! Instead of giving grudgingly, He wants us to be excited. He wants us to have fun giving. I ask you, does "hilarious" describe your giving? Or, does the first part of this verse describe your giving — "grudgingly," or of necessity?

How often do we see people in a typical church service giving laughingly and happily as the collection plate is passed? In the church to which my wife and I belong, we sometimes applaud when we give our offering. I believe we should do this all the time. If we really understand God's laws of prosperity, our time of giving will always be a time of cheerful rejoicing.

Times when we give should be the greatest times of our lives. As always, this is completely opposite to the world's way. Most people think the times when they "get" are the happiest of their lives. Why should we not give cheerfully if we know our money is going to be put to good use? In addition, if a person knows for certain that God is going to see to it that his or her gift is returned, plus more, who would not be cheerful?

If you put money in a savings account, do you do it cheerfully or grudgingly? When we put money in the Bank of Heaven, we put it in a "bank" greater than any this world has ever known. We put our money in a bank with a better guarantee than any bank in this world. Our "savings account" in the Bank of Heaven is backed by the Word of God. Can we believe Him?

When we fully comprehend His Word and believe it with all our hearts, we will be very, very cheerful when we give.

16
Giving God's Way

Both riches and honour come of thee, and thou reignest over all; and in thine hand is power and might; and in thine hand it is to make great, and to give strength to all.

1 Chronicles 29:12

God's way, as we have already seen, is opposite to the world's way: It is "sow to reap," or "give to get." Our Father's Word gives us specific instructions as to exactly how He wants us to live our lives. He blesses us in exact proportion to what His Word tells us to do. One thing He clearly tells us to do is to give to the poor.

When we have a financial need in our lives, I believe God often allows circumstances to occur so that someone with worse needs comes across our path. Despite problems with our own finances, we can reach out and help that person if we really want to. Do we? If so, we plant seeds that enable God to solve our larger financial problems. If we do not, we fail to plant seeds God wanted so He could provide the harvest to meet our own financial needs.

Also, when poor people cross our path, we should not turn away from them. If we give to them, we will be blessed and never lack.

Blessed is he that considereth the poor: the Lord will deliver him in time of trouble. The Lord will preserve him, and keep him alive; and he shall be blessed upon the earth; and thou wilt not deliver him unto the will of his enemies.

Psalm 41:1,2

He that giveth unto the poor shall not lack: but he that hideth his eyes shall have many a curse.

Proverbs 28:27

As we reach out to help the hungry and those in trouble, this will bring the light of God into our lives When we do this, the Lord will guide us continually and supply us with all good things, including good health.

Feed the hungry! Help those in trouble! Then your light will shine out from the darkness, and the darkness around you shall be bright as day. And the Lord will guide you continually, and satisfy you with all good things, and keep you healthy, too; and you will be like a well-watered garden, like an ever-flowing spring.

Isaiah 58:10,11 TLB

God's Word tells us that when we give to the poor, we are actually lending to Him, and He will pay us back. How can we lend money to anyone with better credit than God? He has the best credit rating in the entire universe! This is a loan with a guaranteed return. We know God pays abundant rates of interest.

He that hath pity upon the poor lendeth unto the Lord; and that which he hath given will he pay him again.

Proverbs 19:17

Graciously giving of what we have to help the poor is a way of serving the Lord. He will repay those who do this. On the other hand, we should not give to every "down and outer." Many times this will hurt them more than it will help. God does not want us to be a "soft touch" for anyone with a "sob" story. We should seek the Lord's will before giving or lending money.

A good man sheweth favour and lendeth: he will guide his affairs with discretion.

Psalm 112:5

When we give money to the genuinely poor and needy, we actually receive a two-fold blessing:

First, we know we are helping people who desperately need help, and we know this is the Lord's wish: **Bear ye one another's burdens, and so fulfil the law of Christ** (Gal. 6:2).

Second, we are not actually spending anything when we do this. We are sowing seeds that will produce a harvest. (Gal. 6:7.) If we really comprehend these principles, we will give freely to help the poor of the world.

Your Faith Is a Channel for God

As the Lord continues to give back to us, we will continue to give more and more freely. This will not cost us one cent. The Lord wants to use our faith as a channel through which He can and will pour large amounts of money to fulfill His Great Commission throughout the world. We can help poor people tremendously by giving to them, but we can help them even more by teaching them to apply God's laws of prosperity in their lives.

An old saying says, "If you give a man a fish, you give him one meal, but if you teach him how to fish, you show him how to get food for the rest of his life."

When I was young, I was not only poor but in a seemingly hopeless financial situation with lots of debts and repayment

137

schedules that were more than my annual income. However, I started tithing to my local church and began to study and meditate in God's Word day and night, learning everything I could about God's laws of prosperity.

As I studied and meditated for long hours, I learned from the Bible that God's people who are in debt can get out in two ways: 1) meditate their way out of debt (Ps. 1:1-3; Josh. 1:8), and 2) give their way out of debt (Luke 6:38, 2 Cor. 9:6-8, and Mal. 3:8-11). After many months of darkness, I finally "saw a light at the end of the tunnel."

It is not easy to give when our debts are large, yet this is exactly what we must do. We can give (and meditate) our way out of debt. I know. I did it. This sounds incongruous to anyone whose mind has not been renewed, but it is a principle backed solidly by the Word of God.

Am I saying that, if someone is really "down and out," he should start giving freely to God? This is exactly what I am saying. Many missionaries have testified of teaching God's laws of giving to people in poverty-stricken countries and seeing God bless them abundantly. If God's laws of giving will work in undeveloped Third World nations, they will work in the United States and other countries with much higher standards of living.

When I first started counseling with other Christians on this subject, I used to tell people with financial problems that I thought God would forgive them as they did not have enough to give. That was wrong. I never say this now, after further study into the laws of prosperity and success.

If we tell people they should not give, we are really cheating them out of a harvest which they can only receive by planting their seeds. There are many good Christian books that tell people how to get out of debt, how to manage their budgets, how to stretch their dollars, and so forth. I read several of these books, and some are full of good, logical, practical advice.

However, I have never read one that comes close to putting the proper emphasis on continual giving and constant meditation ahead of everything else. This is what God's Word teaches, and to prosper, we must follow His instruction. Jesus pointed out the importance of giving when it seems as though we cannot give.

> **Then he went over to the collection boxes in the Temple and sat and watched as the crowds dropped in their money. Some who were rich put in large amounts. Then a poor widow came and dropped in two pennies. He called His disciples to Him and remarked, "The widow has given more that all those rich men put together! For they gave a little of their extra fat** (lit. "out of their surplus"), **while she gave up her last penny."**
>
> **Mark 12:41-44** TLB

The dollar amount we give is not as important as the proportion we give compared to what we are able to give.

> **If the (eager) readiness to give is there, then it is acceptable and welcomed in proportion to that a person has, not according to what he does not have.**
>
> **2 Corinthians 8:12 Amp**

Many people give faithfully for a while and then, when financial problems come up, cut down on their giving. If we fall into this trap, we fail a financial test God has allowed to come into our lives. When financial problems come, if we make any changes in our giving, it should be to increase our giving, not to decrease it. In times of difficulty, it is more important than ever to put God first and keep Him first. We certainly are not doing this if we cut down on our giving.

Ten years ago, when my world was falling apart emotionally and financially, I learned "the twin towers of strength" from the fourth chapter of Philippians: **But my God**

shall supply all your need according to his riches in glory by Christ Jesus (4:19) and **I can do all things through Christ which strentheneth me** (4:13). These two verses picked me up off the floor many, many times.

Needs Being Met Depend on Seeds Sown

All over the world Christians are boldly claiming the harvest of Philippians 4:19. However, few of them are careful to first plant the seeds spoken of in Philippians 4:15-18.

When Paul left Macedonia, he reported that only one church gave to his ministry—the Philippian church (Phil. 4:15): In verse 16, Paul mentioned that, when he was in Thessalonica, the Philippians again gave when he was in need; in verse 17, Paul told the Philippians their giving had caused fruits to abound to their "account"; and in verse 18, he told them God was well-pleased with the sacrifices they had made.

Only after these statements did Paul make the famous promise about God supplying all their needs according to *His* riches. The promise of Philippians 4:19 is the *harvest* from seeds planted in Philippians 4:15-18. God promised the Philippian Christians God would supply all of their needs for the same reason He will supply all of our needs: because they gave freely.

If we have sowed the seeds of giving, this verse of scripture tells us that God Himself will supply all of our needs. He is our Source — not our jobs, our savings accounts, or anything else. If we have given properly, we are told that our needs will be met from God's riches.

Another important law concerning finances and prosperity is God's *law of quiet giving*. We should never give so other people will know what we have given. Some people want recognition for being great givers. Scripture warns us against this.

140

"Take care! Don't do your good deeds publicly, to be admired, for then you will lose the reward from your Father in heaven. When you give a gift to a beggar, don't shout about it as the hypocrites do — blowing trumpets in the synagogues and streets to call attention to their acts of charity! I tell you in all earnestness, they have received all the reward they will ever get. But when you do a kindness to someone, do it secretly — don't tell your left hand what your right hand is doing. And your Father who knows all secrets will reward you."

Matthew 6:1-4 TLB

If we want to be admired because of what we have given, the recognition of others will be our only reward. If we give without fanfare, our Father in heaven will know and reward us. Our Father also wants us to give wisely. We should be as careful where we plant our "seeds" as farmers are where they plant seeds. If any kind of seed is not planted in fertile soil, it will not grow. Or, if it does grow, it will not produce much harvest.

In Luke 8:5-8, Jesus told a parable of a sower who sowed seed in four places: by the wayside, on a rock, among thorns, and on good ground. Only the seed that fell on good ground took root, sprang up, and produced a bountiful harvest. This is true in the spiritual realm as well as in the agricultural realm.

It is very important for us to prayerfully ask where we should plant seeds. We should always seek the Lord's will before we give. Luke 6:38 says the Lord uses men to give to other men. He might intend to use us to give to a specific person or organization — one reason we should seek His will before giving.

As mentioned earlier, I believe tithes should go to the local church — the storehouse — the place where we are fed spiritually on a regular basis. However, offerings can go to any number of places. Often, it is not easy to decide on this, as we are besieged with requests from many different ministries.

Our Father does not want us to complicate our giving. He wants us to keep it simple: **... He that giveth, let him do it with simplicity ...** (Rom. 12:8). When we are besieged with requests to give to Christian television programs, radio programs, and many organizations that contact us through the mail, God does not want us to be confused: **For God is not the author of confusion, but of peace ...** (1 Cor. 14:33).

I used to be frustrated by all of the requests I received, but as the years have gone by, I have learned to give more and more as God's Holy Spirit leads me. I give less and less as an emotional response to the barrage of requests from many seemingly good Christian causes. However, I lay my hands on every request I receive and pray for that organization.

I also believe Christians should plan to continue serving the Lord financially after they have gone to Heaven, as well as make provisions for our families after we die. I have done this with life insurance. I also have arranged my life insurance so part of it will be used after I die to continue to give money I definitely would have given if I had lived.

We should leave "our" money so it can not be squabbled over after our deaths and not used for the Lord's purpose. As a result of improper planning, many Christians have allowed "their" money to be used for purposes they would not have agreed to while they were still alive? We must not allow this to happen.

17

How To Receive From God

With good will doing service, as to the Lord, and not to men: Knowing that whatsoever good thing any man doeth, the same shall he receive of the Lord, whether he be bond or free.

Ephesians 6:7,8

We have studied God's laws of giving in detail. Now it is time to study God's laws of receiving. Many Christians have learned how to give, but do not know how to receive. Receiving also is not "automatic." When we give, God does not automatically rain blessings down from the skies.

If we want to receive from God, we must find His laws of receiving, then study and meditate on them, and apply them in our lives. Let us review the receiving end of some promises we have discussed in previous chapters:

Luke 6:38 told us we can receive **in good measure, pressed down, and shaken together, and running over**; Second Corinthians 9:6 told us we can **reap bountifully**; and Malachi 3:10 told us God will open up the windows of heaven and pour out such a great blessing **that there shall not be room enough to receive it**.

Many Christians are receiving only a "trickle" of God's promised blessings instead of the over-flowing abundance promised in His Word. Why is this? I believe it is because many Christians know and apply God's laws of giving, but do not know and apply His laws of receiving.

Are you planting ample financial seeds and failing to receive abundantly? If so, God tells us what we should do.

> **Now therefore thus saith the Lord of hosts; Consider your ways, ye have sown much, and bring in little: ye eat, but ye have not enough; ye drink, but ye are not filled with drink; ye clothe you, but there is none warm; and he that earneth wages earneth wages to put it into a bag with holes. Thus saith the Lord of hosts; consider your ways.**
>
> **Haggai 1:5-7**

God's Word clearly speaks of people who "have sown much yet have brought in little" in return. Therefore, an abundant return obviously is not automatic. We do not *automatically* receive bountifully just because we sow bountifully.

If we are sowing abundantly and not receiving abundantly, what does God's Word tell us to do? Our Father tells us twice to "consider our ways." We need to consider what we are doing, if we are sowing seeds bountifully and not receiving bountifully. Let us take a good look at what we *should* do after we sow seeds.

What does a farmer do after he sows his seeds? Does he just sow the seeds and then forget about them? If he does, he is not going to receive a very good harvest. The successful farmer does a lot more than that. After the seeds are sown, he cultivates the crop, fertilizes and waters it, and clears out weeds.

The return from seeds can vary greatly; it all depends on how good the soil is and how effectively it is cultivated. The same principles apply in the financial realm. After planting our financial seeds, we must cultivate them.

We must continue to study and meditate constantly in God's Word. We must constantly express our faith in an abundant return by our words and our actions. We must not block God by lack of faith or lack of patience, no matter how bad a situation may appear. Lack of patience blocks more Christians from receiving from God than many of us realize.

A farmer would not dream of planting seeds and expecting an immediate harvest. We cannot rush this process. God's laws of sowing and reaping always take time. God has a time for everything: **To every thing there is a season, and a time to every purpose under heaven** (Eccle. 3:1).

It takes a certain amount of time to grow tomatoes.

It takes a certain amount of time to grow corn.

It takes approximately nine months for a baby to be born.

God's Word says to **cast thy bread upon the water; for thou shalt find it after *many* days** (Eccle. 11:1). The word *bread* means anything of substance to us, such as money, time, abilities, and so forth. *Water* refers to people who have needs.

The first part of this verse says, "Give money, time, and abilities to people who have need of them." The second part says God will give back to us when *His* time is right — not ours.

The Harvest Takes Time To Mature

We will receive our harvest "after many days." Many of us are expecting a return when our seeds have not had time to take root, grow, and produce a harvest. Our Father told us in 3 John 2 that He wants very much for us to prosper "even as our souls prosper." The key to God's prosperity is in our souls.

145

Jesus told us, **In your patience possess ye your souls** (Luke 21:19). If we are to prosper under God's laws of prosperity, we must be patient. God does not lie. All of His promises are real. We will reap — if we are patient. We cannot rush God.

The carnal part of us — our old natures programmed with the world's thinking — wants answers, and it wants them now! We must counteract this tendency by developing ourselves spiritually to have the strength and patience to wait for the harvest.

> **And let us not be weary in well doing: for in due season we shall reap, if we faint not.**
>
> **Galatians 6:9**

God's Word tells us we will reap *if*. In other words, reaping is conditional upon patience, on whether or not we get tired of waiting and give up. If we do, we negate God's promise of reaping. Faith and patience go together. The book of Hebrews has a lot to say about the subject of faith and, on at least three occasions, faith is tied into patience:

> **That ye be not slothful, but followers of them who through faith and patience inherit the promises** (Heb. 6:12). **And so, after he had patiently endured, he obtained the promise** (Heb. 6:15). **For ye have need of patience, that, after ye have done the will of God, ye might receive the promise** (Heb. 10:36).

We will not receive bountiful returns, if we are "slothful," lazy and unwilling to pay the price. We must show both faith and patience, if we expect to receive from God. We must work hard studying and meditating in His Word, if we expect to develop faith to the point where we will receive blessings from Him.

We must be certain we do not throw away our confidence in God because of lack of patience. We develop this patience by trusting in the Holy Spirit within us. If we really trust, patience is only one of the fruits we receive.

> **But when the Holy Spirit controls our lives he will produce this kind of fruit in us: love, joy, peace, patience, kindness, faithfulness, gentleness and self-control.**
>
>

Galatians 5:22-23 TLB

Our Father wants us to be single-minded. Our faith must be firm. If we do not get a prompt answer, we must not begin to wonder and doubt. Wavering indicates unbelief and shows we really do not expect to receive from God.

> **But let him ask in faith, nothing wavering. For he that wavereth is like a wave of the sea driven with the wind and tossed. For let not that man think that he shall receive any thing of the Lord. A double minded man is unstable in all his ways.**
>
>

James 1:6-8

I have studied God's laws of prosperity for many years, and I know them well. Nevertheless, I still experience seasons of financial difficulty. When this happens, I do not waver in the least. Instead, I have learned to increase my meditating and to show faith by increasing my giving. When everything looks bad, I have learned to open my mouth and confess that God will provide abundantly just as He has promised.

> **So let us seize and hold fast and retain without wavering the hope we cherish and confess, and our acknowledgment of it, for He Who promised is reliable (sure) and faithful to His Word.**
>
>

Hebrews 10:23 Amp

If we are not receiving an answer, we need to speak out the promises of Joshua 1:8, Psalm 1:1-3, Malachi 3:10-11, Luke 6:38, 2 Corinthians 9:6-8, and many others. We need to praise God and thank Him for supplying abundantly. We must "stick to our guns." Too many Christians waver and begin to speak their doubts aloud.

This negative confession cancels the results that would have been forthcoming, if they had continued to cultivate their crops with faith and patience. We must not doubt God's Word. Our words and actions should constantly show our faith in God.

We should boldly claim the return from our tithes and offerings, saying, "I have given freely and, because I have given freely, my Father gives back to me. You say this in Your Word, Father, and in Jesus' name, I thank You for this return."

Weeds Can Choke Out Your Harvest

The farmer has to clear out the weeds in his garden. We clear out the weeds in the spiritual realm by boldly confessing the promises of God in spite of circumstances trying to choke out our harvest. If we really believe we are going to receive from God, we should talk and act exactly the way we would talk and act if we had a guaranteed Certificate of Deposit (CD) that will mature in time to meet all of our needs!

God's Word is a much stronger assurance than any worldly promise to pay. We see this clearly in the example of Jesus Christ. Jesus *knew* the bread and fish would be there when He had to feed the multitude. He *knew* the coin would be inside the fish's mouth when money was needed to pay taxes. He *knew* the net would come up full when He told the fishermen to put it down after a night of fruitless fishing. This same certainty of God's provision is available to us today.

We have all the Old Testament promises that Jesus had, plus all of the New Testament promises. The same Holy Spirit who lived inside Jesus Christ 2,000 years ago lives inside us today. He is as willing and able to provide abundantly today as He was then. The only variable is the faith and patience of Jesus compared with the faith and patience you and I exhibit today.

While we are waiting for our "crop" to come in, we must cultivate it by continuing to believe and by continually confessing the promises of God. We need to *water* our seeds with constant, unwavering faith and patience, refusing to let the *weeds* of doubt and discouragement choke off our harvest.

Our Father does not want us to limit Him in any way. He knows no limits. The only limits are those that we impose through lack of belief in His promises: **. . . all things are possible to him that believeth** (Mark 9:23). We can block Him through lack of faith on our part.

Our Father has given us complete freedom of choice and is not going to force Himself upon us. He will act according to our faith. If our doubtful words and actions show we do not believe we will receive, lack of faith blocks Him from providing for us abundantly as He wants to do. We should expect to receive. Constant faith enables God to give much more abundantly to us.

Many people fail to receive from God, because they think it is wrong to believe for a return from their giving. Where in God's Word does it say that? Virtually every one of God's instructions on giving is combined with a promise of receiving. If God Himself places an emphasis on receiving, why should we feel there is anything wrong with expecting to receive?

All Christians should release their faith for a great return, not to "feather their own nests," but to finance worldwide Christian revival. Every Christian should want to receive — not just for his or her own needs, but as a channel for God to use to meet the needs of others. Even when we prosper, we must be willing to be a channel that God can bless others through.

There is absolutely nothing wrong with "giving to get" if the purpose of "getting" is to spread the gospel throughout the world! Instead of being wrong, it is our *obligation* to learn how to "give to get" and to act in faith upon what we learn. It is wrong to give selfishly, but not wrong to give believing.

Rags to Riches

Money constantly given is like a clear, bubbling brook —
always fresh and new, cool and refreshing. Continual giving,
backed by unwavering faith and patience, activates God's laws
of receiving and puts us in His perfect will for our finances.

18
Heavenly Laws of Banking and Investment

... And you will always be rich enough to be generous.

2 Corinthians 9:11 NEB

In the previous chapters, we have touched all of the bases on tithing and giving:

• We have talked about why God wants us to prosper through following His laws of renewal, study and meditation, belief, confession, and obedience.

• We have discussed God's laws of sowing and reaping, His laws of tithing and giving, and His laws of receiving.

Now we are ready to pull all of this together as we look at God's laws of banking and investment. We are going to talk about a bank most financial experts on this earth have never heard of: the Bank of Heaven. We are going to talk about investments never listed on the New York Stock Exchange.

God's banking and investment laws are very different from the world's banking and investment laws. The primary difference is that the banking and investing we do in the world's system will benefit us only during our lifetime on earth. The banking and investment laws we will discuss in this chapter also will benefit us during this lifetime. More importantly, however, these transactions will benefit us in eternity.

Every dollar we spend on ourselves on earth perishes as we spend it. However, every dollar we give to God is deposited to our accounts in the Bank of Heaven. Our accounts there can be used while we are on this earth, yet also will be available for eternity.

We are able to open accounts in the Bank of Heaven when we are in good standing with this bank based upon the reference of Jesus Christ. We receive this good standing by accepting Him as our Lord and Savior. This enables us to obtain a "passbook" in the Bank of Heaven. We make deposits and withdrawals in this account following God's laws of banking.

The Bank of Heaven has definite rules just as banks on earth have rules by which they operate. We cannot conduct transactions in a bank on earth unless we follow its procedures. The Bank of Heaven is no different. We must follow God's laws of banking to put money into His bank and to get money out of His bank.

We make "deposits" by giving money to God. Those deposits are in a bank from which our funds cannot be stolen, a bank where our funds will not be affected at all by worldly economic conditions, and a bank that pays interest rates beyond our human conception.

An understanding of God's laws of banking and investment will revolutionize anyone's financial thinking. Once you realize God has a set of financial laws that transcend the earthly realm, you will be motivated to spend hours and hours studying and meditating on those laws in order to learn everything you possibly can about how they work.

Just think how we could transform this world if, by learning and applying God's laws of prosperity, millions of Christians gave hundreds of billions of dollars to God's work! Instead of being spent on temporary, worldly pleasure, this money would be used for eternal, spiritual purposes. As we have seen already, God's laws are exactly the opposite from the way we think with our carnal, worldly minds.

God says, "The only things you get to keep through eternity are the things that you give away." (2 Cor. 9:6-8.)

If we give this money away as God leads us to give it, every bit of what we give will be deposited into our accounts in the Bank of Heaven. God's Word says He wants us to use our money to help others. Jesus said to the rich man who asked how to enter the Kingdom of Heaven:

> **... If thou wilt be perfect, go and sell that thou hast, and give to the poor, and thou shalt have treasure in heaven: and come and follow me.**
>
> **Matthew 19:21**

> **Tell them to use their money to do good. They should be rich in good works and should give happily to those in need, always being ready to share with others whatever God has given them. By doing this they will be storing up real treasure for themselves in heaven — it is the only safe investment of eternity! And they will be living a fruitful Christian life down here as well.**
>
> **1 Timothy 6:18-19 TLB**

We instinctively want to "store up" treasure, and this is fine with God as long as we store it up in the right place. Instead of hanging tightly onto "our" money here on this earth, our Father wants us to give it freely and cheerfully. We will "lay up treasure in Heaven" in exact proportion to the degree we give freely to others of ourselves and "our" money on earth.

Store Up Money in God's Bank

Jesus emphatically warned of the dangers of storing up money on earth:

Lay not up for yourselves treasures upon earth, where moth and rust doth corrupt, and where thieves break through and steal: But lay up for yourselves treasures in heaven, where neither moth nor rust doth corrupt, and where thieves do not break through nor steal: For where your treasure is, there will your heart be also.

Matthew 6:19-21

I believe the "moth" and "rust" and "corruption" Jesus spoke of are the inflation, high interest rates, and self-centered tendencies of the world's economic system. These cruel and negative influences are destroying the life savings of people who have depended upon them.

Who are the "thieves" Jesus said will break through and steal the money that we store up on earth?

The answer is obvious: God's Word tells us these thieves are Satan and his evil spirits: **The thief cometh not, but for to steal, and to kill and to destroy** (John 10:10). Satan is a thief, and he will steal from us in every way he can while we are here on earth. Two of his favorite devices are to try to influence us to spend "our" money on selfish desires or to store it up to provide ourselves with worldly security.

Satan cannot steal what we have deposited in the Bank of Heaven, because he cannot get to it. Inflation, high interest rates, and other economic uncertainties that plague savings accounts here on earth have no effect whatever on the Bank of Heaven. In 1 Timothy 6:7, we are warned against trusting in *uncertain* riches, the riches of this world subject to the ravages of inflation, recession and unemployment.

Instead, God wants us to trust in our "certain riches," the riches we have on deposit with Him. Have you given freely to God for many years? If so, then you have a sizable account in the Bank of Heaven. If not, it is not too late. Now is the time to start following God's laws of prosperity with a definite program of tithes and offerings.

As our worldly economy gets worse and worse, this will become more important, because God's laws will provide for us during the remainder of our lives on earth and throughout our lives in heaven. There is nothing wrong with setting money aside for a "rainy day," if we put it in the right bank!

If and when the stock market fails, or inflation goes wild, or anything else happens to cause our man-made economic system to crumble, our money will still be there in the Bank of Heaven, untouched by any of the calamities of the world's economic system.

If we have given freely of our money here, we can go to the Bank of Heaven whenever we need to make a withdrawal. None of us would hesitate to make a withdrawal from a bank on earth where we had money on deposit. We would go to that bank with complete confidence. It is no different when we do business with the Bank of Heaven. As long as we have made deposits through tithes and offerings, the money is available to us.

How do we get this money out of our account in the Bank of Heaven?

We do it by releasing our faith — by presenting our "faith check" to the Bank of Heaven. We do this by going to this bank *in Jesus' name* — this is the "key" that opens the door to our heavenly account. We then tell our Father we need a certain amount and request this amount with the same faith and confidence as if we requested a withdrawal from a worldly bank.

155

Our withdrawal request will be honored to the exact degree of our faith. Many people never make this request: **Ye have not, because ye ask not** (James 4:2).

God's laws of banking tell us that we will not be able to withdraw money from the Bank of Heaven for selfish reasons: **because ye ask amiss, that ye may consume it upon your lusts** (James 4:3). If we need to withdraw from that heavenly account, we can — as long as our prayer (our request for withdrawal) is in line with God's will for our lives. When we ask according to God's will (His laws), He will hear and grant our request.

You may be thinking your "checking" account in Heaven does not draw interest like an earthly bank. However, this is another area where God's bank is far better than any world bank. Your "account" in Heaven is not only a checking account for use on earth, but a savings account (for eternity), and it pays a high rate of interest.

> **And this is the confidence that we have in him, that, if we ask any thing according to his will, he heareth us: and, if we know that he hear us, whatsoever we ask, we know that we have the petition that we desired of Him.**
>
> **1 John 5:14,15**

19
How To Apply God's Laws

He who is generous to the poor lends to the Lord;
He will repay him in full measure.

Proverbs 19:17 NEB

God's laws of prosperity are for us to use on earth. We will not need these laws of prosperity in heaven. Everyone will be prosperous in heaven.

> **For this commandment which I command thee this day, it is not hidden from thee, neither is it far off. It is not in heaven, that thou shouldest say, Who shall go up for us to heaven, and bring it unto us, that we may hear it, and do it?**
>
> **Deuteronomy 30:11,12**

These laws are very clear. Will you study them? Will you apply these laws during the remainder of your life here on earth? Many people will say these laws will not work. If fact, some religious people will tell you these laws will not work! However, our Father in heaven has said they *will* work and **there hath not failed one word of all his good promise** (1 Kings 8:56).

Every one of the laws of prosperity in this book is based

upon instructions from God's Word. Do not be influenced by people who have never studied and meditated day and night on this subject or stepped out in faith as a result of their study and meditation. Try these laws for yourself.

Pay the price of continual study and meditation. Dare to believe God. Put God's laws of prosperity to the test.

There is only one thing on earth that can stop God's children from prosperity and that is us! This book contains everything any of us will ever need in order to be financially successful regardless of the world's economic condition. It also contains the principles to enable us to prosper in every other area of our lives.

However, none of these facts will have any lasting effects upon your life unless you take definite, specific steps to actually put these laws to use. If you do not do this now, you will soon forget this material. Studies have proven conclusively that a message read or heard only once is almost completely forgotten within 30 days.

The only way to retain these laws of prosperity is to study them and meditate on them constantly and then to apply them in your life. This is not easy. It is hard work. God's laws of prosperity will not do you any good until this information is transferred from these printed pages into your mind and down into your heart and, then, comes out of your mouth. After that, you must act in faith upon these laws.

Diligent study and meditation is required in order to put these laws into effect. In my experiences as a Bible teacher and motivational speaker and in counseling with many Christians, I have found that few Christians are willing to pay the price of constant study and meditation that God requires in 2 Timothy 2:15, Psalm 1:1-4, and Joshua 1:8.

I have laid the foundation for you by digging out many verses of scripture on God's laws of prosperity. I advise you to go back to the beginning of this book and read it again with pen in hand. Underline material you wish to retain. Write notes in the margin. Put an asterisk (*) next to material that is especially important to you. Draw lines or blocks around verses of scripture and other material on which you want to meditate.

Studying Is More Than Just Reading

One of the big differences between studying and reading is that studying requires us to "mark up" with a pen or a pencil the material we are studying. Follow these helpful steps:

• Look up every verse of scripture in your own Bible and see it with your own eyes in God's Word.

• Mark them in your Bible by drawing a rectangle, underlining them, or marking them with a Bible highlighter.

• The next step is to summarize all key points on 3-by-5 cards. Each verse of scripture should be capitalized or underlined so that it stands out.

• Now you are ready to start meditating on God's laws of prosperity. Follow the procedures that were explained earlier. Take one card at a time and carry it with you all day long. Spend a few minutes alone in the morning meditating on the information on that particular card. Think how the scriptural laws on the card apply to your life. Continue to meditate on this throughout the day.

Meditate on this information while you are dressing and washing and brushing your teeth. Perhaps you can place this card on the dashboard of your automobile while you drive to work. Turn this information over and over in your mind throughout the day when you have a break, on your lunch hour, and when you are driving home.

Continue in the evening. While you are meditating on this material throughout the day, open your mouth and speak God's

Word with your lips. Do this over and over. I have seen few Christians who actually open their mouths and continually speak the Word of God. Meditation must include the constant speaking of God's Word as an integral part of God's laws of prosperity.

As you go through the process of meditating on these verses of scripture and speaking them with your mouth, go slowly. Do not rush. Wait on the Lord. Turn these great laws over and over in your mind. Do this slowly, thoroughly, and thoughtfully. As this process continues day after day, week after week, and month after month, your mind will become more and more renewed to God's laws of prosperity.

One at a time, these great laws will drop from your mind into your heart. Soon, your heart will be overflowing with our Father's great truths. They will "explode" deep down inside of you. You will constantly see new shades of meaning in scripture verses that you thought you understood completely. You will constantly come across new levels of awareness of how our Father wants us to live our lives Do not ever stop this process of daily meditation.

The more we learn, the more we realize how much there still is to learn. God's laws are infinite. We will never come close to learning them all. It is overwhelming to even contemplate the sum total of all that is contained in the Bible. As the process of study and meditation goes on, you must put these laws to work by giving cheerfully and freely of yourself and "your" money.

Happiness comes from doing what we know God wants us to do: **If ye know these things, happy are ye if ye do them** (John 13:17).

As we look again at Joshua 1:8 (the only scripture that tells us what to do in order to be both prosperous and successful), we again see the three-point checklist that tells us that we should: 1) meditate day and night in God's Word, 2) speak God's Word continually with our mouths, and 3) actually do everything God's Word tells us to do.

After all of the study and meditation, after speaking God's Word constantly with our mouths, we then must do what our Father tells us to do.

In this book, I have tried to include everything you need to know about God's laws of prosperity. I pray fervently that you will be willing to pay the price to learn these laws and apply them in your life. God will bless you abundantly if you do.

Appendix A:

Selected Scripture Promises for Prosperity and Success

Beloved, I pray that in all respects you may prosper and be in good health, just as your soul prospers(3 John 2 NAS).

. . . The Lord be magnified, Who delights in the prosperity of His servant (Ps. 35:27 NAS).

. . . The things which are impossible with men are possible with God (Luke 18:27).

Be strong . . . Keep the charge of the Lord your God, walk in His ways, keep His statutes, His command-ments, His precepts, and His testimonies . . . that you may prosper in all that you do and wherever you turn (1 Kings 2:2,3 Amp).

If they obey and serve him, they shall spend their days in prosperity, and their years in pleasures (Job 36:11).

. . . They that seek the Lord shall not want any good thing (Ps. 34:10).

A generous man grows prosperous, and he who refreshes others will himself be refreshed (Prov. 11:25 NEB).

Wherefore thou art no more a servant, but a son; and if a son, then an heir of God through Christ (Gal. 4:7).

He who is generous to the poor lends to the Lord; he will repay him in full measure (Prov. 19:17 NEB).

The Spirit Himself bears witness with our spirit that we are children of God, and if children, heirs also, heirs of God, and fellow heirs with Christ . . . (Rom. 8:16,17 NAS).

"If you can?" said Jesus. "Everything is possible for him who believes" (Mark 9:23 NIV).

I can do everything through him who gives me strength (Phil. 4:13).

A man who loves pleasure becomes poor; wine and luxury are not the way to riches (Prov. 21:17 TLB)!

. . . Meditate on it day and night, that you may observe and do according to all that is written in it; for then you shall make your way prosperous . . . and have good success (Josh. 1:8 Amp).

. . . The desire of the righteous will be granted (Prov. 10:24 NEB).

. . . What things soever ye desire, when ye pray, believe that ye receive them, and ye shall have them (Mark 11:24).

And all things, whatsoever ye shall ask in prayer, believing, ye shall receive (Matt. 21:22).

If ye shall ask anything in my name, I will do it (John 14:14).

The Lord is my shepherd, I shall not want (Ps. 23:1).

Nay, in all these things we are more than conquerors through him that loved us (Rom. 8:37).

. . . They who seek the Lord shall not be in want of any good thing (Ps. 34:10 NAS).

God is not a man, that He should lie, Nor a son of man, that He should repent; Has he said, and will He not do it? Or has He spoken, and will He not make it good? (Num. 23:19 NAS).

For ever, O Lord, thy word is settled in heaven. Thy faithfulness is unto all generations . . . (Ps. 119:89,90).

. . . There hath not failed one word of all his good promise . . . (1 Kings 8:56).

... "But the Word of the Lord abides forever" (1 Pet. 1:25 NAS).

... For with God all things are possible (Mark 10:27).

For you know the grace of our Lord Jesus Christ, that though He was rich, yet for your sake He became poor, that you through his poverty might become rich (2 Cor. 8:9 NAS).

Instruct those who are rich in this present world not to be conceited or to fix their hope on the uncertainty of riches, but on God, who richly supplies us with all things to enjoy (1 Tim. 6:17 NAS).

But my God shall supply all your need according to His riches in glory by Christ Jesus (Phil. 4:19).

Wisdom and knowledge have been granted to you. And I will give you riches and wealth and honor ... (2 Chron. 1:12 NAS).

... And you will always be rich enough to be generous (2 Cor. 9:11 NEB).

The blessing of the Lord brings riches and he sends no sorrow with them (Prov. 10:22 NEB).

He that spared not his own Son, but delivered him up for us all, how shall he not with him also freely give us all things (Rom. 8:32).

The grass withers, the flower fades, But the Word of our God stands forever (Isa. 40:8 NAS).

Both riches and honor come from Thee, and Thou dost rule over all, and in Thy hand is power and might; and it lies in Thy hand to make great, and to strengthen everyone (1 Chron. 29:12 NAS).

But you shall remember the Lord your God, for it is He who is giving you power to make wealth, that He may confirm His covenant ... (Deut. 8:18 NAS).

... I am the Lord your God, who teaches you to profit, Who leads you in the way you should go (Isa. 48:17 NAS).

... How blessed is the man who fears the Lord, Who greatly delights in His commandments.... Wealth and riches are in his house, And his righteousness endures forever (Ps. 112:1,3 NAS).

Furthermore, as for every man to whom God has given riches and wealth, He has also empowered him to eat from them and to receive his reward and rejoice in his labor; this is the gift of God (Eccl. 5:19 NAS).

So keep the words of this covenant to do them, that you may prosper in all that you do (Deut. 29:9 NAS).

An arrogant man stirs up strife, But he who trusts in the Lord will prosper (Prov. 28:25 NAS).

He did not spare his own Son, but surrendered him for us all; and with this gift how can he fail to lavish upon us all he has to give (Rom. 8:32 NEB).

Then shalt thou prosper, if thou takest heed to fulfil the statutes and judgments . . . (1 Chron. 22:13).

And he shall be like a tree planted by the rivers of water, that bringeth forth his fruit in his season; his leaf also shall not wither; and whatsoever he doeth shall prosper (Ps. 1:3).

Delight yourself in the Lord; And He will give you the desires of your heart (Ps. 37:4 NAS).

The Lord will open for you His good storehouse, the heavens, to give rain to your land in its season and to bless all the work of your hand . . . (Deut 28:12 NAS).

Poor is he who works with negligent hand, But the hand of the diligent makes rich (Prov. 10:4 NAS).

And God is able to make all grace abound to you, that always having all sufficiency in everything, you may have an abundance for every good deed(2 Cor. 9:8 NAS).

He who gives to the poor will never want, But he who shuts his eyes will have many curses (Prov. 28:27 NAS).

"Give, and it will be given to you; good measure, pressed down, shaken together, running over, they will pour into your lap. For by your standard of measure it will be dealt to you in return" (Luke 6:38 NAS).

He who shuts his ear to the cry of the poor will also cry himself and not be answered (Prov. 21:13 NAS).

With good will render service, as to the Lord, and not to men, knowing that whatever good things each one does, this he will receive back from the Lord, whether slave or free (Eph. 6:7,8 NAS).

Christ redeemed us from the curse of the Law . . . in order that in Christ Jesus the blessing of Abraham might come to the Gentiles . . . And if you belong to Christ, then you are Abraham's offspring, heirs according to promise (Gal. 3:13,14,29 NAS).

For you are all the sons of God through faith in Christ Jesus (Gal. 3:26 NAS).

For no matter how many promises God has made, they are "Yes" in Christ. And so through Him the "Amen" is spoken by us to the glory of God (2 Cor. 1:20 NIV).

We do not want you to become lazy, but to imitate those who through faith and patience inherit what has been promised (Heb. 6:12 NAS).

Jesus said, "I tell you this: there is no one who has given up home, brothers or sisters, mothers, father or children, or land, for my sake and for the Gospel, who will not receive in this age a hundred times as much . . ." (Mark 10:29,30 NEB).

. . . Trust the Lord completely; don't ever trust yourself. In everything you do, put God first, and he will direct you and crown your efforts with success (Prov. 3:5,6 TLB).

Commit thy way unto the Lord; trust also in Him; and he shall bring it to pass (Ps. 37:5).

Yea, the Almighty shall be thy defence, and thou shalt have plenty of silver (Job 22:25).

For there is one God, and one mediator also between God and men, the man Christ Jesus (1 Tim. 2:5 NAS).

But thanks be to God, Who gives us the victory — making us conquerors — through our Lord Jesus Christ (1 Cor. 15:57 NAS).

Blessed be the Lord, who daily loadeth us with benefits . . . (Ps. 68:19).

If you consent and obey, you will eat the best of the land (Isa. 1:19 NAS).

And I will give you the treasures of darkness, And hidden wealth of secret places, In order that you may know that it is I, The Lord . . . (Isa. 45:3 NAS).

But seek ye first the kingdom of God, and his righteousness; and all these things shall be added unto you. Take therefore no thought for tomorrow: for the morrow shall take thought for the things of itself. Sufficient unto the day is the evil thereof. (Matt. 36:33,34).

Honor the Lord with your capital and sufficiency [from righteous labors], and with the firstfruits of all your income; . . . So shall your storage places be filled with plenty . . . (Prov. 3:9,10 Amp).

You are from God, little children, and have overcome them; because greater is He who is in you than he who is in the world (1 John 4:4 NAS).

Bring ye all the tithes into the storehouse . . . and prove me now herewith, saith the Lord of hosts, if I will not open you the windows of heaven, and pour out a blessing, that there shall not be room enough to receive it (Mal. 3:10).

If you then, being evil, know how to give good gifts to your children, how much more shall your Father who is in heaven give what is good to those who ask Him (Matt. 7:11 NAS)!

The thief cometh not, but for to steal, and to kill, and to destroy. I am come that they might have life, and that they might have it more abundantly (John 10:10).

"Truly I say to you, whatever you shall bind on earth shall have been bound in heaven; and whatever you loose on earth shall have been loosed in heaven" (Matt. 18:18 paraphrased).

What shall we then say to these things? If God be for us, who can be against us (Rom. 8:31)?

. . . As it is written, the just shall live by faith (Rom. 1:17).

We live by faith, not by sight (2 Cor. 5:7 NIV).

But without faith it is impossible to please him: for he that cometh to God must believe that he is, and that he is a rewarder of them that diligently seek Him (Heb. 11:6).

But let him ask in faith without any doubting, for the one who doubts is like the surf of the sea driven and tossed by the wind. For let not that man expect that he will receive anything from the Lord (James 1:6,7 NAS).

For verily I say unto you, That whosoever shall say unto this mountain, Be thou removed, and be thou cast into the sea; and shall not doubt in his heart, but shall believe that those things which he saith shall come to pass; he shall have whatsoever he saith (Mark 11:23).

"Verily, verily, I say unto you, whatsoever you shall ask the Father in my name, He will give it you (John 16:23).

If you abide in me, and my words abide in you, ask for whatever you wish, and it will be done for you (John 15:7 NRSV).

"Ask, and it will be given to you; seek, and you will find; knock, and the door will be opened to you. For everyone who asks receives; he who seeks finds; and to him who knocks, the door will be opened" (Matt. 7:7,8 NAS).

"Until now you have asked for nothing in My name; ask, and you will receive, that your joy may be made full" (John 16:24 NAS).

I will do whatever you ask in my name, so that the Father may be glorified in the Son. If in my name, you ask me for anything, I will do it (John 14:13 NRSV).

This is the confidence we have in Him, that if we ask anything according to His will, He heareth us; and if we know that He hear us, whatsoever we ask, we know that we have the petitions that we desire of Him (1 John 5:14,15).

. . . I know that God will give you whatever you ask of him (John 11:22 NRSV).

And whatever we ask we receive from Him, because we keep His commandments and do the things that are pleasing in His sight (1 John 3:22 NAS).

Now to him who by the power at work within us is able to accomplish abundantly far more than all we can ask or imagine, to him be glory . . . (Eph. 3:20,21 NRSV).

"Do not fear, for I am with you; Do not anxiously look about you, for I am your God. I will strengthen you, surely I will help you,

Surely I will uphold you with My righteous right hand" (Isa. 41:10 NAS).

"My covenant I will not violate, Nor will I alter the utterance of my lips. Once I have sworn by my holiness; I will not lie . . ." (Ps. 89:34,35 NAS).

. . Heaven and earth will pass away; my words will never pass away (Mark 13:31 NEB).

Jesus Christ, the Messiah, [is always] the same, yesterday, today, [yes] and forever — to the ages (Heb. 13:8 Amp).

Appendix B:
Have You Entered
Into the Kingdom of God?

You have just read a complete summary of God's laws of prosperity. These are laws that our Father has written for His children, those human beings who have entered into His Kingdom. As I mentioned before, however, these laws and promises are only good for those who have accepted Jesus Christ and become reborn children of God.

Have you entered into the kingdom of God? Jesus said:

> **Verily, verily, I say unto thee, except a man be born again, he cannot see the kingdom of God . . . Ye must be born again.**
>
> **John 3:3,7**

It is very clear there is only one way to enter into the Kingdom of God, and that is to be "born again." We do not enter into God's Kingdom by church attendance, by teaching Sunday School, by baptism, by confirmation, or by living a good life. Jesus paid the price for every one of us to enter into God's kingdom, but this is not automatic.

In order to become a born-again Christian, first of all, we must admit that we are sinners. (Rom. 3:23, James 2:10.) We

171

must admit there is absolutely no way we can enter into God's Kingdom based upon our own merits. Next, we have to genuinely repent of our sins. (Luke 13:3, Acts 3:19.) After this admission of sin and repentance there is one additional step that must be taken in order to become a born-again Christian.

> **For if you tell others with your own mouth that Jesus Christ is your Lord, and believe in your own heart that God has raised Him from the dead, you will be saved. For it is by believing in his heart that a man becomes right with God; and with his mouth he tells others of his faith, confirming his salvation.**
>
> **Romans 10:9-10** TLB

Many people know Jesus died for our sins. However, knowledge is not enough. Intellectual agreement is not enough. In order to be born again, we have to accept Jesus as Savior in our hearts, not just in our heads. God knows exactly what we believe. (1 Sam. 16:7, 1 Chron. 28:9, Heb. 4:13.)

We must believe in our hearts that Jesus Christ is the Son of God, that He was born of a virgin, that He died on the cross to pay for our sins, that He rose again from the dead, and that He lives today. In order to be a born-again Christian, Romans 9:9,10 says we must believe this in our hearts, but also open our mouths and tell others we believe. This confirms our salvation.

We were born naturally on the day our mothers gave birth to us. We must have a second birth — a spiritual birth — to enter into God's Kingdom.

> **For you have a new life. It was not passed on to you from your parents, for the life they gave you will fade away. This new one will last forever, for it comes from Christ, God's ever-living message to men.**
>
> **1 Peter 1:23** TLB

The following prayer will cause you to become born again, if you believe this in your heart and then tell others of this belief:

Dear Father, I come to you in the name of Jesus Christ. I am genuinely sorry for my sins, and I ask for your mercy. I believe in my heart that Jesus Christ is Your Son born of a virgin, that He died on the cross to pay for my sins, that You raised Him from the dead, and that He is alive sitting on Your right hand today. I trust in Him as my only way of entering into your kingdom. I confess now to you, Father, that Jesus Christ is my Savior and my Lord, and I will tell others of this decision now and in the future. Thank you, Father, in the name of Jesus, Amen.

You have been reborn spiritually. You are brand new in the spiritual realm: **Therefore if any man be in Christ, he is a new creature: old things are passed away; behold all things have become new** (2 Cor. 5:17). Now that you have a new, recreated spirit, you are ready to study, understand and obey God's laws of prosperity and all of His other laws. This will transform your life on earth and you also will live forever in heaven.

A Request to Readers

Has this book helped you? If so, would you be willing to tell others so that this book can help them?

Many people are naturally skeptical about the advertising claims for a book such as this. This is why we use a large number of testimonials from satisfied readers in our advertising for this book. If this book has helped you, I would appreciate it if you would write to me in care of the address below.

Please tell me in your own words how this book has helped you and why you would recommend it to others. Include as much information as you can. Also, we will need your written permission to use any part or all of your comments, your name, and the town or city in which you live. (We will not use street addresses and will use only initials for your name.) Thank you for helping others.

TOM LEDING
TOM LEDING MINISTRIES
4412 S. HARVARD
TULSA, OK 74135

More Inspiration
From Tom Leding

Who Said That? will inspire you to reach beyond your present circumstances to be the best you can be. This dynamic collection of daily motivational messages and key scripture verses will challenge and encourage you. Start at any time of the year, and reach for this book any time you need a lift.

Here is a sample of *Who Said That?*:

If Christ is kept outside,
    something must be wrong inside.

Revelation 3:20
Behold, I stand at the door and knock: if any man hear my voice, and open the door, I will come in to him, and sup with him, and he with me.

Many men forget God all day,
    but ask Him to remember them at night!

To order *Who Said That?* or additional copies of *Rags to Riches*, call **918-748-8200** or fax **918-748-8228** or write to:

Tom Leding Ministries
4412 S. Harvard
Tulsa, OK 74135

The cost of each book is $10.00.